THE WHOLE BUSINESS OF BEANS:

HOW TO MAKE COFFEE YOUR BUSINESS.

STELLA PERRY

© 2019 How to Make Coffee Your Business.

All rights reserved. No part of the book may be reproduced in any shape or form without permission from the publisher.

This guide is written from a combination of experience and high-level research.

Even though we have done our best to ensure this book is accurate and up to date, there are no guarantees to the accuracy or completeness of the contents herein.

ISBN: 978-1-953714-03-9

Reviews

Reviews and feedback help improve this book and the author. If you enjoy this book, we would greatly appreciate it if you could take a few moments to share your opinion and post a review on Amazon.

Contents

Roasting Brewing and More. How to Enjoy Coffee Beyond Your Morning Routine — 11
Introduction — 13
History and Origins of Coffee — 19
    History — 20
    Geographical Origins and Spread — 20
The Coffee Making Process — 21
    How it's Grown — 22
    How it's Harvested — 24
    How it's Processed — 25
The Coffee Trade — 27
    Traditional Coffee Consumerism — 29
    Fair Trade Coffee — 31
    Environmental Concerns and Practices — 32
How Coffee is Roasted — 37
    What is Coffee Roasting? — 38
    Types of Heat Used in Coffee Roasting — 39
    How to Tell if Coffee has Finished Roasting — 40
    Different levels of Roasting — 40
    Purchasing a Roaster — 42
    How to Roast Raw Coffee Beans in a Roaster — 43
    Roasting Safety — 43
    Tips and Tricks During and After Roasting — 44
Roasting Coffee at Home — 47
    Where to Buy Green Coffee Beans — 48
    Items You'll Need — 50
        For oven roasting — 50
        For popcorn popper roasting — 51
    Oven Roasting — 51
    Popcorn Popper — 53
    Cooling and Waiting — 55
How to Buy and Store Coffee — 57

Whole Bean vs. Ground	58
Whole coffee beans	59
Ground coffee beans	60
Roasting Date	59
Roaster Information	62
Origin	63
Storage Options	65
How To Taste Coffee	67
Breathe it In	68
Sip Slowly	69
Take a Drink	71
Consider the Flavor Palate	72
Grinding Coffee Successfully	75
Choose the Right Grinder	77
Standard Burr Grinder	77
Bladed Grinder	77
Conical Burr Grinder	78
Hand Crank Grinder	78
Choose the Right Grind Level	78
There are three kinds of grinds	79
Grinding Coffee Without a Grinder	81
Hammer	81
Mortar and pestle	81
Rolling pin	82
Blender	82
Knife	82
Methods of Brewing	83
Drip Filters	84
French Press	85
Pour Over	86
Turkish Coffee	87
Espresso Machine	88
Percolator and Cowboy Coffee	89

Choosing the Right Water for Brewing	91
Soft vs. Hard Water	92
Filtered Tap Water	93
Bottled Water	94
Reverse Osmosis Water	94
Experience Espresso:	97
Not All Beans are the Same	
How is Espresso Different from Coffee?	98
Choosing the right Espresso	102
How to Brew Espresso	102
Combining Espresso and Milk	105
Lattes	106
Cappuccinos	107
Macchiatos	108
To make a traditional Espresso Macchiato	111
To make an American macchiato	111
How to Make Latte Art	113
What You Need	114
Easy Designs to Try at Home	115
Helpful Hints	116
Expanding Your Horizons	119
Coffee-Based Drinks	120
Coffee-Based Desserts	122
Conclusion	127
From a Great Dream to Grand Opening:	
How to Start Your Very Own Coffee Shop	**129**
Introduction	131
Step 1: Creating a Business Plan	135
What are you going to sell?	136
Where are you going to get it?	138
Who is your staff?	139
Who is your clientele?	140

What makes your business special?	141
Review local laws and health criteria	142
A Note About the Next Steps –	144
A Brief Pep Talk	144
Step 2: Do the Math	145
What tools and resources will you need to help you?	145
How are you going to pay for it all?	149
Something Borrowed	150
Making New Friends and Investors	153
Step 3: Create the Space	155
Renting Vs. Buying	156
The Search for the Perfect Spot	158
Location Concerns	159
Finding the Perfect Price Point	160
Asking All the Right Questions	162
Making "Cents" of Your Space	163
Looking Out	165
Make Sure It's on the Up-And-Up	166
Step 4: Time to Go Shopping	168
Construction First	168
Go with the Flow	170
Define Your Style	171
The Big Supplies	173
Appliances Big and Small	175
An Important Reminder and a Second	176
Pep Talk:	176
Step 5: Bringing in the Product	177
Who You Serve Is What You Serve	177
A Snack to Suit the Crowd	178
Considering the Overall Menu	180
Sourcing Coffee	181
Creating Vs. Assembling Vs. Purchasing	182
On the Topic of Waste	186

Step 6: The Wild World of Marketing	188
Sign Here	189
Www. You're Going to Build a Website. Com	189
Follow Us On…	194
Important Things to Avoid on Social Media	197
The Method of Our Forefathers	198
All the Right Stuff	198
Step 7: The Hiring and Staffing Process	201
An Important Note about Labor Laws	201
Determine Who Does What … and When	202
Hire Carefully and Confidently	204
Learning All There is to Know	210
Be Demanding	212
Step 8: Planning for the Big Day	214
Setting the Stage	214
The Final Walkthrough	216
Planning Your Grand Opening	217
What Will Make Your Day Special?	218
Special Deals for a Special Day	220
What Do You Need When You Need a Helper?	221
Be Prepared	222
Business as Usual	224
Conclusion	226

ROASTING, BREWING AND MORE

How To Enjoy Coffee Beyond Your Morning Routine

Stella Perry

Introduction

Have you ever wanted to learn more about coffee or expand your coffee horizons a little more?

If so, you've come to the right place. Whether you're a coffee aficionado or you're just getting started in the world of enjoying your morning brew, we've got all the information you need to learn about coffee from bean to cup—and beyond.

WHAT IS COFFEE?

The word "coffee" can either refer to the coffee plant, the coffee bean, or the drink that is made from this bean. However, most of the time, this term refers to the drink.

Coffee is made by first harvesting the beans of the coffee plant. From there, the beans are dried, processed, and roasted to the perfect temperature to create different roasting strengths and flavors. These beans are then brewed along with hot water to create the beverage that we all know and love.

There's a lot more to coffee than simply that cup you reach for every morning. In this book, you'll learn everything you've ever wanted to know about where coffee comes from, how it's made, and what you can do with the beans once you buy them.

So let's get started!

History and Origins of Coffee

Coffee has been around for a long time. In fact, it dates back all the way to the 1400s, and may have even been around earlier than this. In this chapter, we'll take a very brief look at the history and origins of this classic drink.

HISTORY

Many scholars believe that coffee has existed for much longer than written record shows, and it's thought to have had its origins in Ethiopia. Early written documentation also points to Yemen as one of the first locations where coffee was introduced, although it didn't take long for it to make its way throughout the Middle East and onward. As explorers from Europe began traveling to the Middle East, they were introduced to coffee and brought it back to their own shores as well.

Even in its early days, coffee was consumed in coffee houses as well as in private residences. In this way, coffee has always been at the center of social experiences. Unfortunately, this also caused some religious leaders to believe the drink was satanic, leading to several bans on coffee in different parts of the world.

GEOGRAPHICAL ORIGINS AND SPREAD

Although there's no way to know for sure when coffee was first used as a drink, many myths surrounding this beverage claim that it was discovered by a Sufi (Islamic mystic). According to legend, he witnessed birds with an excess of energy, and decided to try eating the beans they had been consuming to get the same energy for himself. From there, the first understanding of coffee and its properties was born.

Coffee's popularity eventually spread to Egypt and throughout the Middle East, and it soon took off in India, Persia, and Africa too. For a long while, it was largely related to religious practices, particularly in Islamic nations. Soon after, it became popularized in Italy, Asia, and the Americas as well. Despite its ban for some time by the Catholic church, it nevertheless hung on and eventually became the widespread and beloved drink that it is today.

> "Coffee has always been at the center of social experiences ever since it was first enjoyed."

The Coffee Making Process

The coffee making process

begins with farmers who grow the beans, it's more complicated than that. It takes a professional to know and understand coffee plants well enough to make a living from their production. However, even the casual coffee consumer can benefit from a little extra understanding of what it takes to grow and harvest coffee before it's sold to importers or exporters. In this chapter, we'll take a quick look at how coffee is grown, harvested, and processed in order to get it ready to sell and eventually make its way to the shelves of markets and cafes around the world.

HOW IT'S GROWN

There are two different types of coffee plants, which actually grow on shrubs or trees, although one is much more commonly recognized and widely used than the other. *Coffea robusta* is the lesser-known of the two. It is most commonly grown and used in Africa and Vietnam, and it has a much more bitter and rich flavor than the other type of coffee. Although only about 30% of the coffee sold and consumed worldwide comes from the robusta plant, some countries are starting to catch on to its unique flavor. In some instances, both types of beans are brewed together to provide a twist on the classics.

The other type of coffee plant is *Coffea arabica*, which is much more widespread. If you look at just about any bag of coffee beans, you're likely to see the word "arabica," as this is the type of plant your beans probably come from. Arabica beans account for 70% of coffee sold worldwide, and they have a much milder flavor than that of the robusta plant. When discussing coffee roasting, brewing, and tasting throughout this book, we will be referring to the arabica bean unless otherwise specified.

Coffee grows in an area called the bean belt, which has the perfect (more tropical) climate for growing these plants. The plants cannot grow nearly as well in other parts of the world, so their production is fairly limited. The plants were traditionally cultivated in the shade beneath taller trees to encourage them to grow as healthy and as large as possible, and to increase the production of coffee beans per plant. However, as the demand for coffee has increased around the world, sun tolerant plants have emerged. A significant characteristic of coffee beans from sun tolerant plants is that sunlight reduces the incidence of fungal disease which can beset the plant and reduce crop yield.

Coffee beans are initially green when they first appear. If left unpicked, they will eventually turn yellow and then red. They are most commonly picked after they have turned a deep shade of red. Typically it takes two to three years for a given coffee plant to grow beans.

HOW IT'S HARVESTED

Harvesting coffee is a labor-intensive job that takes a lot of work and effort to accomplish. The harvesting stage itself accounts for most of the overall coffee making process. When the beans first come in green, they are latter picked by hand when they are ripe. This is a very time-consuming task, since the coffee shrubs are so large that finding all the beans on a given plant can be tricky. It is uncommon, however, for coffee beans to be harvested by machine, since doing so can severely harm the plants themselves and can also damage to the surrounding rainforests. Because coffee growing areas are often mountainous, only in very flat locations can beans be harvested by machine.

Coffee beans are usually harvested once per year, although this can vary depending on the location and the size of the farm in question. In some parts of the world, the climate is so conducive to coffee growing that plants will bear fruit twice per year instead of just once, such as Colombia, Ethiopia and Kenya.

When coffee is harvested by machine, it's usually done by strip picking. This process strips the fruit of the coffee bush from its branches all at the same time. When hand picking occurs, however, the beans are only picked when they are ripe beans, so the selection process can be more customized. In handpicking situations, pickers are assigned a specific plant to work on for a few days, and then they rotate to a different plant. This gives the beans on each plant a chance to ripen and be harvested at the right time, and it also makes it easier for all of the beans to be examined for readiness.

Once the picking day has ended, the individual picker's product for the day is weighed before being sent off to be processed. A skilled picker can pick between 100-200 pounds of coffee a day, which results in 20-40 pounds of roasted coffee beans.

HOW IT'S PROCESSED

Since coffee beans begin to spoil once they've been removed from the plants, it's important to start processing them right away after they've been harvested. The most common coffee processing technique is called the dry method, in which batches of harvested beans are allowed to dry by being spread out on a tarp in the sun. While the sun is up, the beans are turned, raked and stirred to allow them all to dry evenly and to prevent any rotting that may otherwise occur. Once the sun goes down, they are covered up to prevent rain or moisture from reaching them.

An important reason for drying beans in the processing phase is to reduce the moisture inside the beans to 11%. Below this level coffee loses flavor, and above it, beans can mold. The dry method of coffee processing can sometimes take many weeks to complete, particularly if it's very wet or humid outside at the time.

The other type of coffee processing is known as the wet method. In this technique, the pulp from the inside of the coffee bean is removed after the beans are harvested. This is performed by a machine that separates the inner pulp from the outer skin. This process produces coffee pulp waste, but in many environmentally-friendly and sustainable coffee farming productions, the pulp is used as a natural fertilizer to help improve the coffee harvest for the next year.

After the bean pulp is removed, the beans are then sorted mechanically based on weight and then by size. From there, they go into containers filled with water, where they soak for a day or two to remove the outside layer of the skin. This effectively ferments the beans, leaving them with the perfect texture for final drying and finishing. This process is not possible in countries where there are frequent water shortages, so it is less common in some parts of the world.

No matter which method is used, the beans are then hulled by machine. They may be machine-polished at this stage as well. The final step is to sort them by weight and size once again, and to throw out any beans that have noticeable flaws. This is usually performed by hand, but it may also be completed by a machine. This decision depends on the specific farm or producer. When the entire process is complete, the end result is green coffee that is ready to be roasted.

The Coffee Trade

It's no secret that coffee is one of the most popular drinks in the world. People around the world love it, and have for a very long time. Because of this, coffee is a vastly important commodity, second only to crude oil. When learning all about coffee, it's important to understand all aspects of this trade, and necessary to acknowledge that there are also favorable and unfavorable elements. In this chapter, we'll break down the coffee trade into simple but thorough sections to help make it easier to see just where your coffee comes from.

TRADITIONAL COFFEE CONSUMERISM

Coffee is made by small companies, farmers, and producers who make up the vast majority of suppliers around the world. These exist largely throughout South America, but they can be found elsewhere too. The coffee growing process is very strenuous and requires a great deal of labor to accomplish. Even so, coffee is regularly traded worldwide and is a valuable commodity, typically produced by developing countries.

World events can lead to the rise and fall of the cost of coffee. When wars and other events occur and impact trade, the price of coffee goes up. Embargos and new trade agreements with developing countries may also affect the price of coffee and lead to price changes. In 1986, when Vietnam began exporting coffee to the United States, it heavily affected the Brazilian coffee industry, which led to some Brazilian farmers giving up their jobs and cutting ties with the coffee-making trade. Of course, this also led to a supply and demand issue that further caused the price of beans to fluctuate.

Local cafés, as well as coffee chains like Starbucks, also affect the price of beans. These stores are able to sell coffee and coffee-based beverages for much higher than the cost of their ingredients and in turn, they pay different prices for the coffee beans they use. Some of these chains and local cafés are committed to buying fair trade coffee, which we will discuss in depth below. However, some are not, and they further affect an already unpredictable market.

As China and Russia began to drink more coffee per year in 2016 and 2017, the price of coffee beans rose once again, and this increase in price is still going on today. This also affects the price of coffee stocks, which can be bought and sold the same as any other type of stock.

The chain of coffee trade starts with the producers (farmers and plantations) that grow and harvest the coffee beans, and then goes to the exporters and importers who handle moving that coffee from one country to another. These exporters and importers have most of the control over the types of coffee varieties that are eventually sold to customers around the world. For example, if the importers have a unique type of coffee bean available but are charging exorbitant prices for it, roasters will be unable to buy it, and so it likely won't see widespread use.

Once it is imported, coffee is then picked up by roasters who process it into a form that can be brewed. Roasters pay wholesale prices from importers for their beans and then mark up the price when they sell the beans to retailers such as coffee companies, markets, and cafés. Because of this, the roasters tend to make the most money out of the whole coffee trade process.

Only after the beans reach the retailers do they finally come to you, the consumer. Coffee has a long journey from bean to cup, and it's not always an easy one. However, it is an interesting one, and it can be beneficial to take some time to stop and think about where your coffee has come from the next time you buy a bag of beans.

FAIR TRADE COFFEE

> *Coffee has a long journey from bean to cup, and it's not always an easy one.*

There are many concerns associated with the production and sales of coffee beans around the world from start to finish. As previously mentioned, many coffee farmers in Brazil and other South American countries have been forced to give up their farms and move into sometimes unpleasant and unsafe conditions because they have been unable to sell their product at a profit for a long time. This issue led to a worldwide focus on fair trade coffee, which is still widely recognized today.

The World Fair Trade Organization defines fair trade as a partnership stating that true fair trading must include "dialogue, transparency and respect," and that it must improve conditions for workers who are negatively impacted by the state of trade and its common practices. Organizations that focus on fair trade products work to encourage positive changes in the climate of the coffee trade while still keeping consumers happy. Fair trade certification can be applied to other products, but coffee is one of the most well-known. Fair trade certification can be applied to other products, but coffee is one of the most well-known, and is also one of the products that made this term well-known.

Fair trade allows the producer of the coffee to communicate with importers and negotiate for his or her own benefit . Producers are paid a flat rate for their coffee beans and in turn, importers and exporters then help them reduce their debt so they can continue to farm their product.

In order to be certified as fair trade, a farm must meet certain regulations. However, this isn't the only step required, and some farms that meet these requirements still cannot be certified as fair trade because they can't afford the high cost of getting the certification. For this reason, there are some people who feel fair trade is not beneficial in the long run, and that it really only helps larger corporations that don't do much to assist smaller farmers.

ENVIRONMENTAL CONCERNS AND PRACTICES

There are many environmental issues and concerns related to the production of coffee. As coffee consumers become more environmentally-minded, these concerns have increasingly come to light. While not all consumers stop to think about the environmental impact of their coffee purchases, many do, and it's important to understand what those impacts may be before making a purchase.

Coffee farms and South American coffee plantations have historically provided a safe and secluded habitat for many species of insects and birds that live within the shade of the coffee trees. These farms are similar to small forests and are important parts of the ecological systems in the countries where they are located. These farms are run using old-fashioned and traditional methods, utilizing waste from the coffee production process as fertilizer and handling pest control with no need for chemicals. They don't use fertilizers, and they also regularly grow banana trees which provide shade to help the coffee trees grow, and to provide food for themselves and their families.

This traditional method of coffee cultivation changed when the United States paid these countries and producers to upgrade their methods to more technologically advanced ones. While these new methods mean coffee can be produced more quickly, they also heavily damage forests as well as plant and animal life throughout the areas. Another serious concern is climate change, which, if it raises the average temperature in coffee-growing area, poses a significant threat to the coffee trade.

Replacing the natural shading of coffee and banana trees with different, modernized growing methods can destroy the habitats of many species of birds and insects that call coffee farms their homes. In addition, the new methods that are used, including sun cultivation, require chemical fertilizers and pesticides in order to work properly. These chemicals contribute to a rise in pollution of the groundwater and surface water at or near coffee farms, and can also lead to further habitat destruction throughout Latin America. As these methods continue to be used, soil quality can diminish, and deforestation can spread rapidly.

This problem persists even today, although it has been widely recognized as an issue for some time. Only in recent years have local governments and others involved in the coffee trade sought to repair the damage caused by the modernization of coffee production. Today, some growers are offering higher prices for farming coffee via environmentally-sustainable practices. Other coffees are allowed to be certified as bird-friendly, organic, or shade-grown to show that they are grown using more eco-friendly methods of growing and harvesting. In the future, many coffee consumers, as well as organizations and corporations, hope to shift coffee farms back to their sustainable roots.

How Coffee is Roasted

Although most people know that coffee beans are roasted before they're sold to consumers, the process by which this happens is not necessarily common knowledge. Understanding your coffee from the ground up can help you better appreciate this beverage every time you take a sip, and learning about the process of coffee roasting can make a big difference in how you enjoy your morning brew. In this chapter, we'll discuss what coffee roasting is, as well as some of the specifics for anyone looking to get started using a roaster.

WHAT IS COFFEE ROASTING?

Coffee roasting is the process by which coffee is transformed from its natural state to one that can be used for brewing and drinking. When coffee beans first begin the roasting process, they are still green, but by the time they've finished roasting, they take on the distinct brown color. Roasting relies heavily on chemical processes that increase the flavor of the bean while somewhat decreasing the caffeine content.

Coffee roasting follows a step-by-step order that sounds simple, but relies on a highly skilled professional roaster to ensure it is handled appropriately to prevent unpleasant tastes in the finished product. First, the beans are sorted to remove any unfit individual beans, as well as any unwanted contaminants that may have made their way into the supply.

Next, the beans are weighed and then taken to the roaster, where they first absorb heat and then give off the heat themselves, cooking thoroughly to the perfect temperature. At the end of the process, the beans are cooled before moving along to the next phase on their journey to becoming coffee.

TYPES OF HEAT USED IN COFFEE ROASTING

There are two types of heat used in coffee roasting: endothermic and exothermic. Endothermic heat, means that the heat comes from an outside source and surrounds the coffee bean, warming it up and cooking it from the outside in. This step is required to begin the roasting process and to help the bean reach the right color and roasting level to achieve the flavor the roaster is looking for. This type of heat continues until the temperature in the roaster reaches about 175 degrees Celsius, or 347 degrees Fahrenheit.

Once this temperature is reached, the coffee beans are then switched to an exothermic cooking process. This means that the beans themselves give off the heat they have absorbed, which causes them to more or less roast each other. At this time, the roaster will likely be carefully monitoring the cooking process to ensure the beans don't get too hot or cool down too much to reach the right flavor and roasting level.

Both types of heat involved in coffee roasting represent a precise process that can easily be thrown off if the temperature ranges get too out of control. This is just one of the reasons why coffee roasting is such a difficult skill to master, and why it takes a lot of practice to learn.

HOW TO TELL IF COFFEE HAS FINISHED ROASTING

One of the most important steps in roasting coffee is determining when it's finished roasting. This takes a lot of practice, but it is possible to get the hang of it. Some very experienced roasters can sometimes tell just by looking at the bean when it's finished, but usually other methods are preferred in order to get a more precise roast.

Another way to tell that coffee is finished roasting is to smell it. Coffee beans will begin to smell like coffee as they roast, and the longer they go, the more coffee-like the aroma will become. Just remember that if they go too long, they'll smell burnt and will have an unpleasant flavor.

The final way to check whether or not your beans have finished roasting is to listen to them. When the roasting process begins, you'll hear a pop from the beans—known as the crack—much like you'd hear from popcorn. This initial pop means the beans have reached the very lightest stage of browning at which they can feasibly be brewed into coffee. However, you'll need to let them go much longer if you want them to reach other roasting levels. They will pop a second time when they've reached the realm of dark roast, so remember that medium roast coffee falls somewhere in between these two pops.

DIFFERENT LEVELS OF ROASTING

Technically, there are three levels of roasting. However, there are many different names and styles of roasts that fall into these three categories. Some of these individual styles differ from each other by just a few short minutes of roasting time, so it's important to be very careful when trying to get a specific taste out of your coffee beans. Keep these categories in mind to help you get a better idea of which roasting names fall into which levels:

» Light roast. This category of roasting includes beans that look dry on the outside and have only popped once. They do not taste like roasted beans yet and have more acidity as well as a higher caffeine content than other roasts, since they are closer to their natural form.

Light roasts include New England roast, cinnamon roast, and moderate-light roast, among others.

» Medium roast. This roasting category has popped once but has been roasted past that point. These beans are also dry on the outside and have a slightly more bitter, roasted flavor than light roasts, but not much. They are less acidic and fall in the middle in terms of caffeine content.

Medium roasts include City roast and Full City roast, among others.

» Dark roast. This type of roast causes the outside of the bean to become shiny and look oily. This is because the oils inside the beans have started rising to the surface. Dark roasted beans will pop twice before they're finished roasting, and they taste much more bitter than the other two types of roasts. These beans have a much lower caffeine content than light roasts do.

Dark roasts include French roast, Vienna roast, and Italian roast, among others.

PURCHASING A ROASTER

Buying a coffee roaster can be a beneficial way to start roasting your beans at home. However, knowing which roaster to pick may be challenging. Here are a few tips to keep in mind when choosing a roaster for your home use:

- » Consider the speed of the roaster. If you need to get the job done fast, you'll want to pick a roaster that works faster than others.

- » Consider whether or not the roaster is meant for beginners. Some are harder to use than others. Choose one that doesn't have a lot of complicated features to make it easier to learn how to work with it.

- » Consider how much customization you want. Some roasters allow you to be very precise with custom settings, while others only allow you to choose between light, medium, and dark roasts.

Consider the amount of beans you want to roast at a given time. You may want to work in small batches so your beans don't become stale before you can brew them, or you may be looking for a large-batch roaster that can handle a lot at once. In general, coffee beans start losing their freshness almost as soon as they're done roasting. Standard advice is to roast and use only as many beans as you will likely consume in a two-week period. This gives you the freshest coffee for maximum enjoyment.

HOW TO ROAST RAW COFFEE BEANS IN A ROASTER

When you use a roaster, the process of roasting coffee beans is fairly simple. However, you'll still need to take time to practice if you want to become truly experienced enough to roast to precise temperatures and flavors. Here is the general process for roasting in a roaster:

- » Follow the instruction manual that comes with your roaster to determine the right amount of beans to place inside, and then fill the roaster to the proper level.

- » Turn the roaster on and roast until the beans have reached the color you're looking for. Remember that this may take some practice to get right.

- » Pour the coffee out of the roaster and let it sit, stirring it a little, to cook it throughout.

- » Cool and store the beans until you're ready to brew them.

ROASTING SAFETY

As with any cooking and food preparation you try at home, it's important to keep a few safety tips in mind. Remember that your coffee roaster is a heated appliance and that the beans themselves will be quite hot when you take them out of the roaster. Handle with care, and do not leave the roaster unattended while it's running. Be careful not to let the cord near water.

Roasting beans release carbon dioxide as they heat, so operate your coffee roaster in a ventilated room and don't cover any fans on the outside of the product. The CO_2 gas from coffee roasting can be dangerous, so be sure it doesn't build up in your home.

Do not open the coffee roaster while it's working. This can cause an increased risk of fire and burns as well as smoke inhalation. It should also go without saying that you should never let children use the coffee roaster.

TIPS AND TRICKS DURING AND AFTER ROASTING

Now that you know a bit about the process of coffee roasting, here are a few tips you can remember to help you make the most of the experience.

» Learn to recognize the smell of the roast you're going for.

» Stay close-by and listen for the first and second pops.

» Don't start with entirely green coffee beans when roasting at home, as they can be harder to roast and may even damage home coffee roasting machines.

» Store your coffee beans in an airtight container in a cool, dark location for best results.

Roasting Coffee at Home

Brewing coffee

Brewing coffee in your home and putting together the perfect cup can be a fun and rewarding experience, especially if you're interested in the world of coffee. However, if you really want to try something new and a little outside the box, you might want to attempt roasting coffee yourself at home instead. If you never realized you could roast coffee in your own home, you're in luck. In this chapter, we'll give you all the information you need to get started with your home coffee roasting endeavors.

WHERE TO BUY GREEN COFFEE BEANS

Unroasted coffee beans, also referred to as green coffee beans, may be hard to find. However, knowing where to look makes it easier to find a good quality batch of green coffee. There are a few steps involved in picking good green coffee.

Choose your beans' region. Region is important to decide on before shopping, as some vendors and stores may separate products based on origin. Others may only offer beans from one location or another, as well.

Beans from Central and South America are good for beginning roasters. These beans offer mild flavors in many varieties that can be used for all sorts of roasting levels and techniques. Beans from Brazil remain a popular choice among new home roasters, particularly because these beans are sweeter than some of the other options out there. Choose a bean from this region for light and medium roasts with a few darker options.

Coffee beans from Indonesia can be a lot more affordable than those from other locations. However, this coffee has a stronger and sometimes bitter flavor, so it may not be for everyone.

You can also try roasting green coffee from other locations. However, the two mentioned here are the most common and easiest to find, so they're better for those who are just getting started.

Stick to arabica beans, especially if you're not very experienced yet. Robusta beans are a lower quality type of coffee and may not have a good flavor. It takes an experienced roaster to know how to bring out the good elements of a robusta coffee bean. However, some blends do contain a portion of these beans, and buying a blend including some robusta can help you save money. For this reason, even some new roasters don't shy away from blends.

If possible, ask the vendor about the specific flavor profile and aspects of the coffee beans you're considering. You may not always be able to find out this information, depending on where you get your beans. When you can, find out about the acidity, body, and taste of the beans.

Decide whether or not you want to buy fair trade, organic, bird-friendly, or other categories of beans. If you can afford to do so, it's a good idea to look for at least one of these options on the label.

You can order beans online, but you probably shouldn't the first time you buy green coffee. It's better to be able to smell and look at the beans before you buy them. If you do order online, be sure to stick to trusted vendors with good reviews and a positive reputation among coffee roasters.

Don't over-purchase, especially for your first time buying. Buy just enough beans to allow you to practice your roasting technique, but not so many that they'll go bad before you can get through them all. This is also a good choice in the event you end up with a bean whose taste you don't really like.

Store your beans in a cool, dry location. Keep them in an airtight container and away from heat and direct sunlight. Make sure to keep them in a place where insects and pests won't be an issue as well.

ITEMS YOU'LL NEED

Gather the needed items before you begin the roasting process. Although some of these are optional, you will need to have most of them on hand to ensure the job is as easy and smooth as possible. There's more than one method of roasting coffee beans at home, so be sure you get the items you need for the right process.

FOR OVEN ROASTING:

- » Oven
- » Baking pan with perforations. Make sure you don't choose a pan with large enough holes that the coffee beans can fall through them.
- » Kitchen timer
- » Wooden spoon or spatula
- » Durable oven mitt for safety
- » Metal strainer

FOR POPCORN POPPER ROASTING:

» Popcorn popper (air style popper with vents on the sides—not on the bottom)

» Bowl for catching bean skins

» Wooden spoon

» Metal strainer

OVEN ROASTING

Follow these steps to learn how to oven roast your coffee beans. This method is not as simple as the popcorn popping one listed below, but it can give you a little bit more control over the way the beans roast, as well as the flavors and aromas you can get from the beans you've chosen.

Depending on whether or not you have an electric or gas oven, the temperature you need to set for preheating may differ. It's recommended to start with 500 degrees Fahrenheit for electric and slightly lower, around 475 or so, for gas. However, you may need to adjust this to get the right roast.

Spread the beans over your baking pan so that they're all touching each other but not sitting on top of each other. Make sure they cover the "floor space" of the pan.

Open some windows and turn on some fans. You should also turn on the ventilation on your oven, but keep in mind this probably won't be enough on its own to take care of the smoke the roasting process will produce. Understand that there's a chance your smoke detectors will go off while you're roasting.

Make sure you can easily get the beans out of the oven and outdoors somewhere to cool when they're finished roasting. You need to lower their temperature quickly when they are finished roasting, so taking them outside is a good option.

After the oven finishes preheating, put the tray of beans in and shut the door. Turn on the kitchen timer and stay close to the oven.

The first few times you roast, check on the beans very frequently at first. If you notice them roasting in one spot more than in others, stir them quickly as needed. Do not open the oven door often and do not leave it open for more than a few seconds at a time.

Listen for the first pop of the beans. This will let you know that the green coffee has reached the point just before the light roast stage. If you don't want a dark roast, you'll need to take them out before you hear a second pop. However, if you want a very dark coffee, you'll need to wait for two pops.

As soon as the beans are the color you want, take them out of the oven and hurry—carefully!—to get them outside for cooling. Place them in a metal strainer and shake them gently to help cool them off and remove the skins from the outside of the beans at the same time.

It usually takes anywhere from ten to fifteen minutes to roast coffee, depending on your oven, your pan, and the roast you're looking for. It may take a lot of trial and error to get this right when using an oven, but with enough practice, you'll be roasting the perfect coffee beans right in your own kitchen in no time.

POPCORN POPPER

It's easier to roast coffee at home in a popcorn popper, although it still takes some getting used to. With a little practice, you can easily learn how to achieve the perfect roast for your coffee using this simple method.

Put your popcorn popper in a place where the smoke won't cause any major issues. Some people like doing this outside or near a window, but your oven's hood fan can sometimes be enough to deal with the smoke, too. Just like with the oven method, expect a lot of smoke and the possibility of your smoke detectors going off.

Check out the manufacturer's recommendations for how much popcorn to put in the popcorn popper at one time. Measure the same weight in coffee beans and place them in the popper.

Set the lid, butter dish, and other pieces of the popcorn popper into place as you would for normal operations. Keep in mind that it is crucial for coffee beans to stay in the popcorn popper longer than it is for popcorn kernels. You may run the risk of melting your butter dish using this method. All popcorn poppers are unique, so use your best judgment when picking one for this task.

Put a bowl or other receptacle under the popcorn chute. This is for catching the skins of the coffee beans as they get thrown off during the process.

Turn the machine on. Stay close-by so you can listen for the first popping sound, the same as you would with the oven roasting method. The same rules apply here too—one crack means you're nearing light roast, while two cracks means you're in dark roast territory. It should take only two or three minutes to hear the first pop.

About a minute after the first pop, check the beans for color and roast. Continue checking frequently until they reach the desired color.

It should take about four minutes for a light or blonde roast and up to seven minutes for a very dark espresso-style roast, with medium and medium-dark falling in between these two times. Do not leave the beans unattended, as the roast color can change very quickly.

Be sure to remove the beans from the machine just before they reach the darkness you're looking for. This will account for further cooking from the inside as they cool down to room temperature and can prevent the beans from burning, especially if you're going for a darker roast.

Place the beans in the metal strainer and stir them with a wooden spoon until they cool down to be warm enough to touch.

> *Be sure to remove the beans from the machine just before they reach the darkness you're looking for.*

COOLING AND WAITING

No matter which means of roasting you choose, you'll need to wait for the beans to cool down before you can finish processing them. This step may be tempting to skip, but it's crucial to making sure your beans taste great and stay fresh.

The biggest reason why you need to cool your beans down quickly is because they will continue to roast from the inside out if you don't. This will quickly cause them to burn and develop bitter, sour tastes that you simply don't want in your coffee. However, they also cannot be exposed to much water at this stage, so there's no way to soak them to cool them off either.

It's widely recommended to use the metal strainer method listed in both guides above for cooling your coffee beans. Stirring the beans and allowing air to flow all around them is a good way to quickly lower their temperature. Doing this outside can help even more.

If it's very hot outside when you roast your beans, you might want to spray them very gently with cold water from a spray bottle. Do not overdo this, and always err on the side of less water if you decide to try it. When you spray the hot beans, you should see the mist from the spray bottle evaporate right away. This will work to keep them cooler without saturating them with water and ruining them.

If all else fails, roast in the morning or at night so you don't have to worry as much about heat. And keep in mind, too, that the humidity outdoors can make it harder to cool down your coffee beans in a timely manner. Don't forget to account for the weather when trying to roast at home.

How to Buy and Store Coffee

Now that you've learned a little bit about what coffee is and where it comes from, it's time to branch out into the realm of purchasing coffee for yourself.

When you go to the store to buy coffee, you may think it's as simple as picking between caffeinated or decaf. However, there are some additional elements involved in the selection of coffee, and choosing a good one that will suit your needs and preferences can be tricky. In this chapter, we'll help you better understand how to buy your coffee as well as how to store it when you bring it home.

WHOLE BEAN VS. GROUND

There are two main types of coffee available for purchase: whole bean and ground. Wherever you choose to purchase your coffee beans, you'll find both options available on the shelves. Some people prefer to stick to coffee that has already been pre-ground before packaging, while others like grinding it themselves at home. There are pros and cons to both of these options, however, and it's a good idea to understand the pros and cons of each so you can make the right choice.

Take a look at the two styles of coffee and consider which one may benefit you the most.

WHOLE COFFEE BEANS

If you buy a bag of whole coffee beans, you're getting a product that's as close to fresh as possible. These beans are still in the state they were in when they left their farm, and they haven't lost much of their flavor yet. They'll still look, smell, and taste as intensely as they did right after they were finished being processed. This is the reason why many consumers prefer to buy their beans whole, so they can enjoy the coffee's flavor as it was intended—straight out of nature and into a cup.

Whole beans are a little more of a hassle than the pre-ground variety, however. When you buy whole beans, you need to think about how to store them to preserve their freshness. The point of having coffee made from whole beans is to enjoy the freshest possible taste every time you brew, so it's crucial to make the right storage decisions to ensure this can happen.

It's also a little more inconvenient to buy whole because you'll need to grind the coffee yourself. This will require a coffee grinder or some other piece of equipment as well as time to take care of the task on a regular basis.

GROUND COFFEE BEANS

As you learned in previous chapters, coffee goes through a lengthy process before it reaches the bean form most consumers recognize. As soon as the beans complete this journey—and once they are roasted—they begin to lose their flavor. In other words, coffee is perishable. The longer it sits on a farm or in a warehouse, the greater the opportunity it has to lose its freshness. Most of the time, coffee reaches buyers before it loses too much of its flavor profile. However, this is not always the case, and ground coffee may suffer the most from the natural aging process.

When coffee beans are ground, their taste and aroma both begin to escape immediately. Coffee that has been pre-ground before packaging is never going to taste or smell quite as nice as whole, fresh coffee beans. For this reason, too, ground coffee may go stale much sooner in your home than whole coffee beans might.

However, ground coffee is much more convenient to purchase, since you don't have to worry about grinding it yourself. If you don't own a coffee grinder or don't have the time to worry about grinding beans regularly, this may be a better option for you.

In the end, the choice is up to you. Some people swear by ground coffee while others only buy whole. There isn't much of a price difference between the two, so there's no budgetary reasons why you may want to pick one or the other. The biggest difference is in the taste, with shelf life and aroma also playing a part. Just remember that you'll need to purchase something for grinding your coffee if you decide to go with whole beans, and you'll need to brush up on your grinding ability as well. (More about coffee grinding later.)

For the best coffee experience, stick to whole beans.

ROASTING DATE

Coffee does not last as long as you might think it does. Many people buy big tubs of pre-ground coffee and keep it in their refrigerator, freezer, or pantry for months, slowly working through it before repeating the process again. Although this method will certainly provide you with a cup of coffee to drink every morning, it's not the best way to go about enjoying your brew. Buying coffee in bulk is not a good option unless you're planning to drink it all very quickly, as it will go bad sooner than you realize. When you want to savor your morning brew, there are better methods.

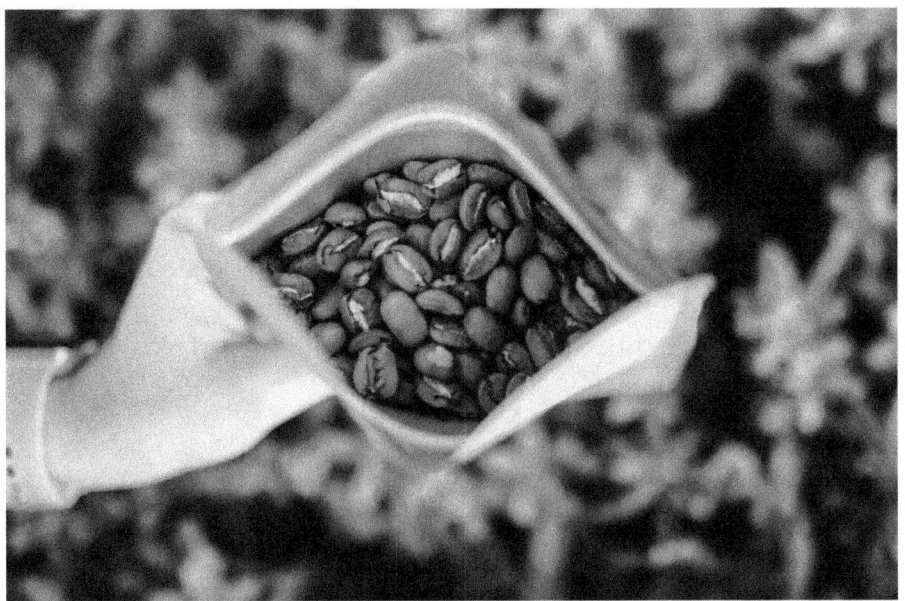

Paying attention to the roasting date on your bag of coffee can help you better keep track of how long it can be used. This date will let you know when the beans finished processing, so you can understand how long they've been sitting on the shelf before making their way to you. You have several months to enjoy the coffee before its flavor will diminish and it will start to taste stale. However, the sooner the better in most cases. As with any type of food, the beans will taste better while they're still fresh and closer to their natural form.

Remember that your coffee will change more after you open its packaging, and it will begin to experience off-gassing at this time. Some types of beans taste better after off-gassing for a few days than they do right out of the brand new bag. Espresso, for example, is better after sitting for about a week-and-a-half in a cool, dry location before you brew it. Beans intended for pour overs (pouring water directly over coffee through a filter into your cup) can benefit from sitting for a few days before you use them as well.

Bags of coffee usually also have an expiration date printed on the packaging. Although you will not get food poisoning from coffee that is past its expiration date, it will not taste its richest anymore. Technically, whole bean coffee can be kept in the freezer for nearly a year after this date, and ground coffee can stay in the freezer for many years with no cause for concern. Although old frozen coffee may do in a pinch, it's not going to give you a great taste experience, so standard coffee wisdom is to buy smaller amounts of coffee and use it up within approximately two weeks for best flavor.

ROASTER INFORMATION

The next step in choosing a good coffee is to take a look at the roaster information printed on the packaging. Sometimes, the brand name and the roaster are not the same thing—particularly if you buy your coffee locally or from a small mom-and-pop store. Even some bigger and more well-known brand names of coffee come from a roaster with a different name, though, so be sure to take your time and look closely for this information. Knowing the roaster responsible for your beans can help you figure out whether or not they're the right beans for you.

Some roasters may be just starting out. If you're thinking of buying coffee from a new roaster, there's no reason not to give it a try. Just remember that it may be lacking in the complexities of a coffee profile created by a roaster who's been at it for several years or more. On the other hand, some roasters may be relatively unknown but capable of providing very high-quality coffee with amazing tastes and smells throughout the experience. Sometimes it pays to branch out and try coffee beans from someone new. There's always some risk with doing this, but it can be well worth a try.

A very good roaster is going to be well-known, at least in the world of coffee aficionados. When you find the name of the roaster responsible for the beans you're considering, look it up online. A quick search will let you know if it's become popular or recognized for its skill and ability with beans. You may also be able to use this information to find out whether or not the roaster has been recognized formally with certifications or awards for product, practices, or both. Some may even be celebrated outside the coffee industry, too.

In some cases, the beans you're thinking about buying may not tell you the name of the roaster. If this happens, there may be one of two reasons. The first possibility is that the name on the bag is the same as the roaster's name. The second, however, is that the roaster may not be well-known enough to get a place on the bag. This is usually common in lower budget coffee, but again, the experience can vary depending on the brand and bag. If the identity of the roaster matters to you, it may be better to skip those coffees that do not provide you this information.

ORIGIN

There are many possible origins of coffee. Beans that come from different locations taste differently due to environmental factors, and some consumers prefer one location's flavors over the others. Choosing the right coffee for your needs may be a little easier when you determine which origins you like the most. A quality bag of beans will tell you somewhere on the packaging where it comes from. If you buy your coffee from a café or a specialty shop, the employees or baristas should be able to give you this information as well.

Some of the most common origins you may find in your coffee enjoyment experiences include the following:

BRAZIL. These coffees have bold flavors and lots of elements in every sip.

HAWAII. This type of bean is lighter and smells more fragrant than other types.

ETHIOPIA. All sorts of coffees come from this region, from light to dark and from mild to bold. They span many tastes and styles.

COLOMBIA. These are milder, lighter roasts than some of the others found worldwide.

KENYA. This type of coffee isn't for everyone, as it can be sour and bitter. However, many people enjoy this unique twist on the classic brew and go out of their way to buy Kenyan coffee beans.

Remember that you may also want to consider environmental friendliness, green practices, bird safety, and fair trade when choosing your coffee. These factors can help you narrow down your selection and pick a product you can feel good about buying with an origin that isn't harmful to the world around you. More and more consumers are reaching for coffees that meet one or more of these requirements, so you may want to take this opportunity to give them a try for yourself, too.

STORAGE OPTIONS

If you've always been the type of person to throw your coffee beans in the freezer without a second thought, here are some tips to help you make better storage decisions.

Buy less coffee at a time to ensure it stays fresh as long as you need it to.

It's okay to keep coffee in an open, room temperature container for a few days. However, after about a week, it will start to degrade in quality, so only do this if you know you'll be using it soon enough.

Keep coffee beans and pre-ground coffee both in airtight, sealed containers. Store them away from sunlight and in a cool, dry location.

When you need to grind beans, only grind enough for the coffee you'll be drinking that day. This way, you can use them while they're still fresh and the taste is optimal.

If you do choose to freeze your coffee, make sure the container you use is completely airtight to prevent freezer burn. This will also keep the coffee from picking up any unpleasant flavors and smells from the freezer and the other food around it.

Plastic and glass containers can both work for coffee, but plastic may cause strange odors after a while.

HOW TO TASTE COFFEE

Did you know

you can practice coffee tasting the same way you'd try wine tasting? Enjoying a cup of coffee can mean so much more than just guzzling it down and moving on to the next activity for the day, but it takes a little practice and know-how to get it right. When you understand the process for coffee tasting, you can learn more about your own preferences and the flavors that stand out to you with every cup. This can also be a nice way to bond with fellow coffee fans and to share your knowledge with others, too.

In this chapter, we'll walk you through the steps you need to take to enjoy a coffee tasting experience unlike any you've ever had before. You can try this with any coffee you have on hand, but you're more likely to find complexities and subtle notes among specialty coffees and those that come from whole beans. With time, you can learn to identify or at least narrow down origins of your coffee based on the way they taste, and you will come to understand more about how to buy and enjoy the beans you love by exploring various coffee tastes.

BREATHE IT IN

You probably already know that taste begins with your nose. When you smell something, it helps you get a better idea of what to expect from the flavor, and it can even help increase the tastes that go along with the food or drink in question. Coffee is no different, and smelling it before you drink it can make a big difference in the way you enjoy your sips. You can start smelling coffee as soon as you open the container of beans, and this is widely recommended as the starting point for the true enjoyment of any brew.

After you smell the beans, grind them according to your preferences and needs. Next, smell the ground coffee once again, and take the time to notice how the aroma has changed as the form of the coffee was altered. The same main notes should still be there, but there will be some elements that mellowed out after grinding and others that came to the front of the profile. This is also a good time to write down anything you might want to remember about what you're enjoying as you smell the first few steps of the coffee, too.

If you're making your coffee as a pour over, wet the grounds a little as per the pour over method. Before you continue, lean in and smell the wet grounds just a little bit. You don't have to take long for this step, as taking too much time will negatively impact the pour over experience. However, you should at least notice the way the grounds change once again when they are exposed to water.

Finally, when the cup of coffee is ready for you to drink it, tilt the cup so that you get a full whiff of the smell and really breathe it in. This last, most important part of the first stage, can get your mouth and tongue ready for the experience of drinking the coffee.

SIP SLOWLY

Most coffee fans and pros look for a handful of flavor types and elements in each sip of coffee. As you begin sipping, take your time and process the taste throughout your whole mouth. Swish the coffee around like you would with wine so you can experience the way it hits each part of your tongue differently. Just as with wine, many specialty coffees are made to evoke different responses depending on how you enjoy them. Here are some of the elements to be on the lookout for:

CLEAN FLAVOR. This means that, when you swallow the coffee, the bitter aftertaste isn't going to hang around in your mouth. Most coffees do leave a little bit of a flavor on the tongue and in the mouth as a whole, but a solidly good cup of coffee shouldn't do this. It should not make your breath stale with coffee taste, and it shouldn't leave you with a sour or smoky feeling in your mouth either. It should leave your mouth feeling clean and ready to move on to another sip or to a bite of your food instead.

ACIDITY. This term refers to any coffees that provide a flavor including lemon, tomato, or blueberry. Although you may not realize it, there are actually a lot of coffee variations that make use of these types of flavors. Some coffees have acidity due to the ingredients used in brewing or processing, while others may get theirs from the weather and climate in the location where the beans are grown. The term acidity, in this case, does not refer to the pH level of the coffee and only describes flavor.

SWEETNESS. Many coffee beans have a sweetness to them, and most of the time, you can even smell it at least a little bit in the whole bean. When you sip the coffee, are you able to locate different sweet sources throughout the flavor profile? Can you find the taste of mocha or chocolate, which is very common in some dark roasts especially? Or are you picking up on honey, caramel, or maple? Just as with acidity, the location and means of production of the beans can affect the sweetness of the coffee, as can the roast and even the grind.

BODY. Another term for this is "mouthfeel," although it's not often used to describe coffee as much as alcohols and liquors. Is the coffee very watery, or does it have a fullness to it when you take a sip? Does it sit in the mouth a certain way, or does it go down smoothly? Can you identify that the coffee is a dark, medium, or light roast simply based on the body, and can you consider the body of the drink when determining how it was ground and brewed too?

TAKE A DRINK

Now that you've taken your time in identifying smells, tastes and textures going on in your cup, it's time to actually sit back and take a drink. You shouldn't sip your way through the entire mug of coffee, but you should give yourself plenty of time to really work through the contemplation of the drink before moving on to the full drinking stage. This way, you'll learn to identify the flavors you like and pick out the ones that aren't working for you very well. In doing this, you'll have a better relationship with coffee and how you drink it, and you'll know what to expect from your favorite beans, too.

When you take a drink of your coffee, there's no need to chug it. In fact, if the coffee is very rich and bold, you may want to avoid chugging it altogether, as it could disrupt your tasting experience. Take a normal drink of the brew and see how the various tones you picked out in the previous step work together. How do they dance with each other, and where do some of the flavors stand out more than the others? Are you still noticing the same tastes you picked up on before, and is the original aroma of the whole bean still making its presence known?

When you get to the bottom of the mug, are some of the grounds still floating there? If so, you may not have chosen the right brewing method or picked the right grind. The coffee should be smooth and consistent throughout the whole experience, and if the last sip is unpleasant compared to the rest, something may need to be tweaked somewhere along the way. This is part of the trial and error of coffee brewing, so don't be discouraged if something went a little wrong.

CONSIDER THE FLAVOR PALATE

Thinking about the flavor palate of your coffee involves asking yourself several questions. These questions can help you determine the different elements involved in both the beans and the brew, and they can also make it easier for you to pick out things you like and dislike in the world of coffee tasting. This way, the next time you go shopping for a new style of beans, you'll know more than just, "I like blonde roasts," or, "I'm not into medium roasts." Here are a few questions to ask yourself at the end of your cup of coffee to finish off the tasting experience:

- » Did I notice more than a couple of flavors going on together? If so, did the flavors work well with each other, or did some of them stick out in a bad way?

- » Did I notice layers of flavoring, or did everything land the same way on my tongue? Were there stages of each sip, or did it feel too repetitive working through the cup?

- » As the coffee got cooler, did the flavor change? If it changed, was it for better or worse? Did it get bitter and taste old after it got colder, or did the flavors become something new and equally enjoyable?

GRINDING COFFEE SUCCESSFULLY

As with most aspects of enjoying coffee, you can handle this one the easy way or the hard way. Sticking to ease and convenience is fine if all you're looking for in your cup of coffee is something to wake you up on your way to work every morning. However, if you truly want to be able to sit back, relax, and relish in that brew, it's going to take more than a quick chop in a coffee grinder to get your beans ready for tasting. By understanding the ins and outs of grinding your coffee beans at home, you can set yourself up for a better result every time you pour yourself a mug.

In this chapter, you'll learn how to pick the right type of grinder for your coffee, as well as what to do if you don't have a grinder at all. You'll also find out which grind level is right for different styles of coffee brewing, even if you're interested in trying less common or more elaborate techniques and methods. This may seem like a lot of complicated information, but with a little practice and learning, you can easily start making coffee that is ground to perfection before you even add water.

CHOOSE THE RIGHT GRINDER

The first step in getting your coffee to the perfect grind every time is to make sure you're working with the proper grinding method. There aren't a lot of different types of coffee grinders out there, but the varieties that are available to you can make a difference in the flavor of the coffee you brew. When you go to the store to buy a grinder, you may be a little overwhelmed by the different selections available. Take a look at our tips below to help you keep track of which kind is which.

STANDARD BURR GRINDER

This is one of the most common types of coffee grinder on the market. It comes in at about mid-range in terms of pricing. The standard type of Burr grinder is the plate grinder, and this variant utilizes two flat disks that spin continually and press together to mash the coffee beans into the right consistency for brewing. These are very precise appliances that can allow you to pick from a wide variety of different levels and settings. However, their biggest flaw is that they get a little too warm and have been known to burn the coffee beans or cause them to taste a little smoky.

BLADED GRINDER

When you think of a coffee grinder, chances are good this is the type you imagine. This is the cheapest style on the market and it is a very basic solution to whole bean grinding needs. All you have to do is fill it with beans, close the lid, plug it in, and let it do its job. It works by rotating sharp blades inside the main housing chamber and cutting up your coffee beans as it does so. You can control the degree of your grind from coarse to fine by the length of time you run the blades. After a bit of practice you'll know how long to operate your grinder to get the grind you like. This type of grinder is a little harder to keep clean, but not overly so—a stiff bristled brush and a damp cloth will do the trick.

CONICAL BURR GRINDER

This is a different style of the standard Burr grinder listed above. It is the most expensive type of home coffee grinder and is generally the best as well. This is an electric product that allows you to set the grind to the level and style you want, push a button, and let the appliance do the work for you. It's easy to keep this type of grinder clean by taking it apart and rinsing or scrubbing the individual pieces as needed, and it's also easy to learn how to use this item, too. It's a great choice for beginners who aren't sure about how to precisely control other options from this list, and it's good for old pros who want to branch out in their coffee experiences too.

HAND CRANK GRINDER

Another affordable mid-range solution is a hand crank grinder. This an old-fashioned product that has started to come back into fashion among some coffee fans. To operate one of these items, you must place beans inside and manually turn the crank. This takes a long time and is rather difficult, so it is not ideal for those who are in a hurry or anyone that doesn't want a workout along with their morning cup. However, when looking for a way to show off to friends and family, or you want to buy a unique present for a coffee lover in your life, this can be a good alternative to other grinders.

CHOOSE THE RIGHT GRIND LEVEL

The next stage of this experience is to choose the right grinding level for the coffee you're making. In other words, you're picking the grind that's right for the type of coffee maker you have. If you don't have a coffee maker and you're planning to brew your coffee using another method, then it's even more crucial to choose the type of grind that's meant for the style of beverage you want to create. This can take some getting used to, but with practice, you'll be able to determine the right method of grinding for just about any type of coffee.

THERE ARE THREE KINDS OF GRINDS:

Coarse: This grind looks like coffee beans that haven't been chopped up very much, and that's pretty accurate. Its appearance is similar to dirt, and individual pieces are all big enough to see. Within broader "coarse" terminology, grounds may be either standard or extra-coarse. Extra-coarse will look even more distinct and have larger chunks than the standard.

Medium: Next up is medium. This looks more uniform in terms of the sizes of the individual pieces, but you can still tell them apart from each other by looking. When you pour it, this coffee looks like sand moving through an hourglass. The pieces should all be more or less the same size. One good way to match a medium grind is to compare it to store-bought coffee grounds. Unless otherwise specified, this type of coffee is almost always ground to medium.

Fine: Fine grinds look and feel similar to sugar. They are hard to tell apart from each other when you look at the finished product, and they may be so fine that they would pass through certain types of coffee filters and products. If you've ever bought pre-ground espresso, chances are good you've come across finely ground coffee at least once. Most espresso beans that are sold already ground to fit into the finely ground category, although some may lean a little more toward medium fine.

There are also another two styles to keep in mind.

SUPER FINE: This grind is extremely fine, but when you rub it between your fingers you can still feel the texture of sugar granules. This is only meant for certain types of coffees and shouldn't be used for the more common variations you're likely to be brewing.

TURKISH GRIND: This method is specifically meant for making Turkish coffee. In this grind, the beans are broken down into a powder with a consistency similar to flour. It is much different than other grinds and isn't really intended for any other type of coffee because of this.

Each method of brewing coffee can be divided into a different grind category.

COARSE: Use coarsely ground coffee for French press and vacuum style coffee makers. This is also the best choice for a percolator.

MEDIUM: Auto drip coffee makers—like the ones you can find in most household kitchens—use medium grinds. You may want to go with a medium to fine grind if your coffee maker has a cone filter instead of a flat one.

FINE: Espresso pots and espresso machines utilize fine coffee grinds. You may also choose a fine grind if you have a conical drip filter, instead of a medium-fine grind. These coffee makers can usually work with both interchangeably.

SUPER FINE: This style is best for espresso machines that require very small granules of coffee in order to function properly.

TURKISH: You should only use this grind for making Turkish coffee, as it's too fine and powdery to work otherwise.

GRINDING COFFEE WITHOUT A GRINDER

What happens when you want to drink freshly-ground coffee but don't want to buy a grinder? Is it even possible to make coffee from whole beans without something to grind it as part of your kitchen appliance ensemble? When you have access to whole beans but not a coffee grinder, you do have options. Take a look at the list below to help you figure out the best way to grind and enjoy your coffee beans even if you don't own a grinder and don't want to purchase one.

HAMMER

If you've never thought of beating up your coffee beans with a hammer, now's your chance to give it a try. This is a somewhat dangerous method, so be careful not to try it on a fragile countertop or table, and take care to keep your fingers safely out of the way. Put the beans on a piece of parchment paper over a sturdy surface. Use the hammer (or a meat tenderizer) to break down the beans to the right consistency. You should get a coarse grind out of this.

MORTAR AND PESTLE

If you're into making your own ground spices at home, you may already have a mortar and pestle. If you don't have one, they're usually more affordable than coffee grinders. Place a small amount of beans in the mortar and crush them with the pestle, twisting as you go to make sure the beans break up as they should. Continue rolling and moving the coffee around in the mortar until it is the right grind for your needs.

ROLLING PIN

Spread some parchment paper over a big cutting board and fold the edges to make a pocket for keeping the coffee in one location. Spread a small amount of the beans out over the paper and use the rolling pin to crush them. Press down firmly while pushing the rolling pin back and forth across the beans.

BLENDER

You can get a grind similar to what you'd find with a blade style grinder by using your blender. Remember, however, that not all blenders have blades that are strong enough to handle coffee beans. Some have a coffee-specific setting, and others are capable of processing coffee but don't specify this. Be sure to read the blender's instruction manual to find out more. It's best to pulse your blender rather than to turn it on a specific setting so you can better keep track of the grind. You should be able to achieve a standard coarse-to-medium finish when you use a blender.

KNIFE

Finally, you can use a knife in a manner similar to the hammer and rolling pin methods if you want to. Put the beans on a sturdy cutting board and spread them out evenly. You should not try to chop the beans, but instead lay the knife on its side and use the flat portion to crush the beans to the grind you're looking for. You can get almost any level of grind from this method, including coarse, medium, and fine. With practice, you may even be able to crush espresso beans to the right texture by utilizing a knife.

Methods of Brewing

Most people know there are several ways to brew a good cup of coffee, but how do you know which one is really right for you? Some people prefer one method over others, and some are happy to change between different methods depending on their mood, day, or time of the year. Familiarize yourself with the most common (and some more uncommon) methods of brewing to easily pick the one you'll enjoy the most. Try choosing different brews as you learn and grow.

DRIP FILTERS

A classic drip filter is ideal for most types of coffee. These are the types of coffee makers you can find in most kitchens (and diners), and they have become so popular for good reason. They brew coffee quickly and can make a very good cup in most instances. They're easy to clean, small enough to fit on most kitchen counters, and aren't nearly as expensive as some of the other choices out there. They come in many varieties, colors, and styles to suit most needs, making them a good all-around choice.

You probably already have experience operating a classic electric coffee maker. Basically, the appliance receives water to a certain volume depending on how much coffee is needed. A paper filter is put in place for holding ground coffee. Water is pumped into the filter, which drips through the ground coffee, and is caught in a carafe below. This product makes a bubbling sound synonymous for many people with waking up in the morning.

These coffee makers can be a great choice for medium grinds. They may seem a little too ordinary, but you can make a very good cup of coffee using this type of product. They are not designed to handle coarse grinds (which can clog up the filter and the machine), nor can they deal with fine grinds (that can simply be pushed through the filter and contaminate the coffee). But for medium grinds, there's no reason to break the bank on complicated machinery. As an added bonus, high-quality water yields even better results.

FRENCH PRESS

The French press is an older coffee making method that has recently seen a comeback in popularity. Coffee is relatively consistent when made in a press. Pressing extracts oils and caffeine content from beans in a more uniform way than other methods, and helps the coffee taste better and wake you up more quickly at the same time. This method isn't for everyone, but it's a good choice for those looking to get a little something different out of their regular cup.

You must use coarse ground beans in a French press to ensure the press works as it should and doesn't become damaged. Place grounds in a press pot along with the correct volume of water. You may need to let it sit for one or two minutes, or you may be able to start pressing right away—be sure to read the manufacturer's instructions to find out for sure. Press the coffee plunger down slowly to force the brewed coffee through the built-in filter and allow it to drip into a receptacle. This takes about four minutes.

If you're looking for a more portable and convenient French press option, you can choose the AeroPress. This product does use a filter and relies on a lot of elbow grease to push the plunger down. It can work in a pinch, but it is a little pricey and may not be ideal for regular daily use. It may also not make as consistent a cup of coffee as the regular press pot can.

POUR OVER

A pour over works in more or less the same way as a classic drip coffee filter, but it is a manual process instead of an electric one. This method is very low cost and is a great solution for anyone who wants to enjoy the full flavor and aroma of a cup of coffee without spending a fortune to make that happen. It's also ideal for people living in smaller spaces who don't have room to devote to larger coffee makers or espresso machines. You can find pour over items for as little as about ten dollars, or you can get nicer ones made of better materials for much higher prices, depending on what you're looking for.

To make a pour over cup of coffee, you must first set up the coffee cone over a receptacle. The cone and receptacle are usually sold together, but not always. The shape and style of the cone, as well as the material it's made of, can make a difference in the way the coffee will taste when it's finished brewing. When the cone is set up and in place, you must then put a filter in place as well. You have to buy the right type of paper filter for the cone you've chosen. Place about three tablespoons of ground coffee in the paper filter inside the cone and make sure it's tapped down into the cone, but not pressed firmly together. Heat water to just before boiling, then pour it gently and slowly over the coffee in the filter. It's best to start pouring a little, stop and wait for the coffee to bubble, and then continue pouring. The coffee will drip through the filter and be ready to drink in about three minutes.

There are many different styles of pour over products you can choose from. Depending on the material and shape you like, you may be able to find some easily, while others can be pricey and tough to come by. Chemex is a very popular choice among pour overs, but it is a little more expensive than most others and relies on a specific type of filter in order to work properly. However, if you want to try the upper end of quality for your next pour over, Chemex is the way to go.

TURKISH COFFEE

Turkish coffee is becoming more and more popular in recent years, and if you've never tried it, then you may want to take time to check it out. This type of coffee is surrounded by ritual and culture, so it can be beneficial to your appreciation of the drink to read up on the background of the brew and learn what it means to those who have been drinking it for centuries. You will need some specific materials and items to make this type of coffee, and it may take a little longer to brew than some other methods.

To begin with, you need very finely ground coffee. You should choose coffee that has been ground so much that it is like powder or flour. Any other type is not going to work. You can grind it yourself or look for pre-ground coffee that is labeled for Turkish coffee purposes.

Add a cup of cold water and a pinch of sugar to a very small saucepan and bring to a boil over medium heat. Take the boiled water off the heat as soon as it boils and add a tablespoon of the ground coffee and a pinch or two of ground cardamom. Stir very gently and then return to the heat. Let it boil once again, and take the coffee off the heat when it starts to foam and bubble on top. Let it settle for a few seconds, then repeat the process, removing the coffee again from the heat when it starts to foam. Pour the coffee out into a small cup and let it stand for a couple of minutes before drinking. This will allow the grounds to sink to the bottom and will make the flavors much more pleasant as well. Do not stir your coffee after you pour it.

ESPRESSO MACHINE

Espresso machines are only intended for use with espresso beans that have been ground to the right consistency for espresso shots. They cannot be used to brew a regular cup of coffee, and trying to do this can damage your machine as well as ruin your drink. If you want to pull espresso shots, then you will need an espresso machine. However, if you don't, then it's better to skip this expensive and complicated piece of equipment.

If you are looking to buy an espresso machine, remember that you can find several models and styles to suit your needs. A true espresso machine is a large piece of equipment that is very expensive and comes with all the bells and whistles you need to make the perfect shot every time. However, it is possible to find much smaller machines that can pull a shot or two of espresso at once and maybe steam milk as well. These machines are usually plenty for home espresso enthusiasts to enjoy.

PERCOLATOR AND COWBOY COFFEE

Coffee hobbyists tend to neglect the percolator as a viable way to brew coffee at home. However, depending on the flavor and style you're looking for in your drink, this may be exactly what you need. Percolators were popular many decades ago, but they're still available if you know where to shop for them, and they can be an interesting and fun addition to a coffee fan's kitchen. Buying a quality percolator is important, as some are made a little bit worse than others and may not provide you with the taste you want. Choose a metal percolator for best results.

To percolate coffee, you first must fill the bottom of the product with enough water to make the volume of coffee you need. Try to get this measurement as exact as possible to prevent your coffee from being too strong or too watered down. Attach the filter to the percolator and put in the right amount of coffee grounds—one tablespoon for about every eight ounces of water. Put the top portion of the percolator on and close the lid. Put the percolator on your stove over medium heat until it is very hot but is not boiling yet. You may need to adjust the heat as you go to keep the water from boiling or the coffee from brewing too fast.

Once the water reaches a point where it's making a few bubbles every now and then, it's ready. Turn off the heat but leave the percolator on the hot burner for about ten minutes (or less if you prefer a milder coffee). Take the percolator apart so you can access the coffee inside. Although this process is a little more involved than some others, it is environmentally friendly and is ideal for camping too.

Cowboy coffee works much like coffee made in a percolator. Make this coffee by putting water in a stovetop pot. The amount of water you choose will depend on how much coffee you want in the end. Boil over medium heat, then remove as soon as it boils. Leave it alone for 30 seconds. Measure out two tablespoons of coffee for every cup and add directly to the pot. Use only finely ground coffee for this purpose. Stir, then let stand for two minutes, and then stir once more. Leave it alone for another two minutes and then drizzle a small amount of cold water over the top. Pour carefully so grounds do not get into the drink.

Cowboy coffee isn't the best or most delicious way to make coffee, but some people enjoy trying it every now and then, especially for a fun twist on the more common methods. It's also a good choice for camping, since you only need a fire and a pot to make a good, strong cup of coffee just about anywhere.

CHOOSING THE RIGHT WATER FOR BREWING

Picking the right water for brewing your coffee is one of the key factors in making the perfect cup. Some types of water simply aren't cut out for coffee brewing. If you're interested in making a cup of coffee the recommended way, you should understand the different water types and issues you may encounter when trying to do so. While there's nothing stopping you from making coffee with water right out of the tap, there are some compelling reasons why you might prefer to choose something of a better quality, and a little more filtered, before you start working on your morning brew.

SOFT VS. HARD WATER

Hard and soft water are both terms that can describe any water with a pH balance other than neutral. While it's always nice to have pH balanced water, most of the time it's not really possible to have it right out of your tap. Most homes have either hard or soft water, and it's important to find out which your home has before deciding whether or not to use your tap water for brewing coffee. Both of these types of water conditions pose different challenges when making coffee, but they can both be rectified as well.

Hard water is another term for water that has a higher mineral content. This water also naturally has a higher pH due to the presence of hard minerals, including magnesium and calcium. If water is only slightly hard, these minerals may actually add to the flavors in the coffee and bring out some of the subtleties a little bit more. Many people prefer to brew their coffee with slightly hard water for this reason. However, if the water is too hard, the calcium and magnesium present within it will build up on your espresso machine or coffee maker and can cause damage over time.

Soft water, on the other hand, has a lower pH and doesn't contain nearly as many minerals naturally. If you use a water softener in your home to soften your water, it may replace these minerals with sodium. Too much sodium in your softened water may make it taste a little salty, which can negatively impact the flavor of your coffee. Using sodium instead of hard water minerals may also make the water—and therefore the coffee you make with it—taste weak and unappealing.

If you must choose between the two, somewhat hard water is better than soft for coffee brewing.

FILTERED TAP WATER

Tap water is the worst choice for brewing coffee, since it's full of unwanted pollutants, contaminants, sediments, and other issues. You shouldn't put it in your coffee maker or espresso machine, as it can eventually cause clogs and damage the inner workings of the appliance. In most places, it's also not very safe to consume the tap water without filtering out at least some of the substances that are found in it.

Using a pitcher filter can help you get enough water for your coffee maker at any given time. These filters can remove chlorine and improve the taste and smell of your water. A sink faucet filter can remove a little more and may be a better option if you make a lot of coffee, or if you want filtered drinking water instead. You can also choose to install an under-sink water filter to help improve the quality of all the water that comes out of the specific sink in question.

Finally, if you really want to improve your home's water, you can put in a whole house water filter. These filter systems come in many different varieties and can remove many impurities as well as bacteria and dangerous substances from your water. They are not cheap, but they can keep you healthier while making your water taste better too. And when your water tastes better, so will your coffee—which is just a nice added bonus.

BOTTLED WATER

Bottled water is a better choice for coffee than tap water is. However, there are some issues to keep in mind when trying to choose the right bottled water for your needs, too. Some bottled waters may be more alkaline than others, and some may contain higher mineral content than others. Some are nothing more than glorified tap water, while others are very high-quality water that is well worth the price—and worth brewing into a cup of coffee every now and then. You may need to practice a little trial and error to find the right bottled water.

You should never use water that is labeled as "distilled" or "purified" for this purpose. Only pick water that says "drinking," "spring," or "artesian" on it. Water labeled as mineral water is also usually safe. And it may go without saying, but don't put sparkling or flavored water in your coffee.

REVERSE OSMOSIS WATER

Reverse osmosis is a water treatment option that takes almost all of the minerals out of the water before drinking. Some people believe this is a better way to treat the tap water in a home, but unfortunately, reverse osmosis also removes the good minerals from the water along with the unwanted ones. This is not only bad for your health, but also bad for your taste buds, as the water may be unpleasant and can lead to a badly brewed cup of coffee. Reverse osmosis water has nothing in it to bring out the natural flavors of your coffee.

Some of the more elaborate reverse osmosis filtration systems on the market will add the desirable minerals back into your water after removing contaminants and pollutants. These are very expensive and hard to come by, though, so chances are good your home is not fitted with one of these filters. If you are thinking of installing a reverse osmosis filter and want to pick something that's better for you as well as for your coffee, choose one that adds the minerals back to the water. Just remember that your coffee may be a little lacking if you use this type of water.

> *Only pick water that says "drinking," "spring," or "artesian" on it. Water labeled as mineral water is also usually safe.*

Experience Espresso:
Not All Beans are the Same

Espresso and coffee—

two of the most popular ways to wake up, start the day, or relax and enjoy some quiet time. No matter how you choose to drink your caffeinated beverage, you probably have a favorite between these two, right? They may seem like they're vastly different from each other, but really, espresso and coffee have many similarities too. In this chapter, we'll explore the ways these two types of beans differ, as well as how to choose the right kind of espresso for your favorite drinks. You'll also learn how to brew espresso at home, whether you prefer to use a machine or stick to a pour over.

HOW IS ESPRESSO DIFFERENT FROM COFFEE?

Espresso and coffee are actually more alike than they are different, even though that may be difficult to believe! Most of the differences are aesthetic ones, in that they affect the appearance, flavor, and smell of the coffee. The beans themselves, however, still come from the same plant as all other types of coffee, and they are effectively the same product. And when it comes to caffeine, the similarities are stronger—a serving of coffee and a proportional serving of espresso have around the same caffeine content. Things get a little different between the two when you consider the brewing method as well as the processing method. Here is a list of some of the ways espresso and coffee are different from one another:

Espresso is brewed much differently than coffee. There are many ways to make a brewed cup of coffee, but when it comes to espresso, the method must include speed and pressure. Water is sent through the ground espresso quickly in order to brew this beverage. This is why you must have an espresso machine if you want to make real espresso. On the other hand, if you want to make a pour over of regular coffee, you need only to gently pour hot water over the ground coffee and allow it to drip into a cup.

YOU CAN MAKE ESPRESSO AS A POUR OVER AS WELL. SOME COFFEE FANS WILL TELL YOU THAT ISN'T "REAL" ESPRESSO, WHILE OTHERS SAY IT IS JUST AS ACCEPTABLE. IN REALITY, THE DECISION IS UP TO YOU, SO FIND THE METHOD YOU ENJOY THE MOST, REGARDLESS OF THE ARGUMENT.

Whereas coffee can be ground to several different consistencies and can come in many roasts and flavors, espresso is more specific. In order to qualify as espresso (and to be able to be brewed in an espresso machine), beans must be ground finely and have an extremely dark roast. If the grind is too coarse, the espresso will not have the full flavor and body it is meant to have. On the other hand, if it's too fine, the coffee will be much too bitter.

IF YOU'RE MAKING ESPRESSO AS A POUR OVER, YOU WILL WANT TO GO FOR A SLIGHTLY COARSER GRIND, SOMEWHERE IN THE MEDIUM RANGE. THIS WILL PREVENT THE COFFEE FROM SEEPING THROUGH THE FILTER DURING THE PROCESS.

Finally, espresso can be used in several types of drinks, while coffee is really only intended for a few options. Coffee can be enjoyed straight (or with milk and sugar), Americano, or iced. There aren't really any other variants on it in terms of drinks you may find on the menu at a café. Espresso, however, can be used to make drinks including cappuccino, macchiatos, flat whites, lattes, and much more. The rich, smooth flavor of espresso pairs well with milk and holds flavors nicely, so it's better suited to these types of drinks than traditional brewed coffee.

CHOOSING THE RIGHT ESPRESSO

Picking a good espresso will help you find a flavor you enjoy working with. And when you choose the right beans for your brew, it will be easier to work through the process of learning to make espresso, too. Anytime you go to a store or café selling espresso beans, you may feel a little overwhelmed by the selection. However, once you get the hang of it, picking the perfect beans will be a snap.

Keep these tips in mind when shopping for beans for your espresso:

All beans can be used for drip coffee, but not all beans can be used for espresso. You can make drip coffee using beans that have been labeled espresso. The term "espresso" on a bag of coffee simply means that the roaster, farm, or company feels that these beans are best used in espresso beverages. On the other hand, if you have a bag of non-espresso coffee beans, you cannot use them in place of espresso. They may not hold up to the brewing method, and they may be too weak to carry the flavor of the milk.

Single origin is more expensive than blends. Single origin coffee is any bean that comes from just one location. A coffee blend is made up of beans from more than one place. Blends are cheaper, because the base bean can be a lower quality or more affordable option, while the beans used to accent and add to the flavor may be higher quality. There is nothing wrong with using either of these options, and it's important to pick the one you like the best. Although single origin is more popular among regular coffee, blends are still the go-to choice for espresso in most situations.

There are many shades of dark roasted coffee. Just because a coffee is dark does not make it an espresso. However, espresso must be dark. You can usually choose a dark bean that's on the lighter side for espresso if you like, but the darker options will yield bolder and more flavorful results. This choice is up to you, but remember that medium and light roasts may not work at all.

The rich, smooth flavor of espresso pairs well with milk and holds flavors nicely

Flavored or unflavored is up to you. Some espresso beans have flavors while others are strictly going to taste like the beans themselves. There's nothing wrong with choosing a flavored bean if you like it. However, remember that traditional espresso is not made with flavored beans, so it's important to choose the right type for the drink and situation. Don't forget, too, that many flavored coffees are not dark roasts.

HOW TO BREW ESPRESSO

The best and most well-known method of brewing espresso is to use an espresso machine. Some of these machines are electric and automated, while others are manual. Some hook into a water supply line while others rely on you to fill the reservoir every time you want to pull a shot. There are so many differences among espresso machines that it's important to read through the instruction manual on yours. This will help you learn the ins and outs of operating your own machine as well as keeping up with its maintenance.

Read through these directions to learn how to brew an espresso shot using the most common variant of espresso machine.

- » Heat up the espresso machine about a half hour ahead of time. Take this time to pour water into the machine if needed and ensure there is a filter in place.
- » Pull a shot of water to warm up the equipment and flush the nozzle.
- » Remove the filter and put it on a digital food scale. Zero out the scale. Add seven grams of ground espresso to the filter.
- » Using a tamp, press the espresso down into the filter to "seal" it.
- » Place the filter into the head of the espresso machine, then turn on the machine.
- » If your machine is not automatic, you'll need to watch carefully. Stop the espresso shot at 20 seconds for best results.

» Your espresso should be turning lightly blonde in color when you stop the shot. When finished, it should be dark on the bottom and have a crema on top. A crema is a short, frothy section you can see when you look at the espresso, similar to the head on beer.

» If you prefer your espresso as a pour over, the method is not all that different from making pour over coffee. Remember, though, that it will take longer to wait for your espresso to brew this way, and that some types of espresso beans may not be strong enough to be used in milk-based coffee drinks when made via pour over.

Follow these directions to brew up a hot cup of espresso using the less common pour over method.

» Heat water to 200 degrees Fahrenheit. Wet the filter slightly.

» Choose a grind that is intended for pour overs instead of a grind for espresso machines.

» Add the ground coffee to the filter and pour in just enough water to cover. Stir gently.

» Wait for the water to stop bubbling, then begin pouring water in the center of the grounds, spreading to the outside in a circle. Continue this for three minutes.

» Your pour over espresso should be ready to drink. Note that you won't see a crema when you brew espresso this way.

COMBINING ESPRESSO AND MILK

Once you have learned the right way to brew your espresso and you know how to pull a shot from your espresso machine, it's time to start branching out with drinks based on this brew. You can start by learning the basics that make up any great espresso beverage. You'll need to perfect the art of pulling the right shot for a given drink, but you'll also need to understand how to handle the milk component in these beverages. In this chapter, you'll learn how to combine milk and espresso in various ways to create some of your favorite café drinks without ever having to leave the comfort of your own home.

LATTES

The quintessential espresso-based hot drink is the latte. If you've ever gone to a café for a specialty drink, chances are good you've tried a latte before. Whether you're a latte connoisseur or this will be your first time experiencing one, you can learn how to put one together easily by following these simple instructions.

A latte contains more milk than most other types of espresso drinks. Traditionally, it is made with whole or 2% milk, but depending on your preferences and health needs, you can make it with any type, including soy or almond milk. A latte is known in some parts of the world as café au lait or grand crème.

To begin, use your espresso machine to pull a single shot of espresso. There's no need to aim for a longer or shorter shot unless you just want to; a traditional shot will work just fine. Pull the shot directly into the cup you'll be using.

If you're going to be using any flavored syrups, now is the time to add them. For a single serving latte, it's best to only use one or two pumps of syrup unless you just want an incredibly sweet drink.

You can also add sugar at this stage and allow it to dissolve in the hot espresso. Try not to over stir the espresso shot. If possible, however, do not use granulated sugar and instead go with liquid cane sugar. This will improve the flavor and consistency of the latte.

Next, pour enough milk into your espresso machine's steaming pitcher to make up the equivalent of at least two shots. You can add more if you're using a larger cup, but don't overdo it too much or the drink is going to taste like milk with a little coffee flavoring.

Steam the milk until microbubbles begin to form. You should listen for the sound of paper tearing when using the steaming wand on your espresso machine, and then continue for a couple of seconds longer.

Use a large spoon to hold the bubbles back while you pour the steamed milk directly on top of the espresso shot and syrup in your mug.

Use the same spoon to ladle the foam bubbles out of the pitcher and onto the top of the drink.

If you're going to be adding latte art, skip the bubbles on top and go straight to the art instead.

IF YOU WANT TO MAKE A FLAT WHITE INSTEAD OF A TRADITIONAL LATTE, YOU CAN FOLLOW THESE STEPS WITH A FEW MINOR CHANGES. WHEN YOU STEAM THE MILK, TRY TO GET AS FEW BUBBLES AS POSSIBLE. AND WHEN YOU POUR THE MILK INTO THE MUG OVER THE ESPRESSO, DO SO CAREFULLY AND SLOWLY SO THAT YOU CAN SEE ONLY A SINGLE WHITE DOT OF MILK ON TOP OF THE BEVERAGE. THIS IS THE SIGNATURE FLAT WHITE LOOK.

CAPPUCCINOS

Americans, and especially those who drink their coffee and espresso from chain cafes instead of locally-owned ones, tend to have the wrong idea of what a cappuccino really is. Some people believe that it is more or less the same thing as a latte, but that isn't really true. A cappuccino may be made from steamed milk and espresso like a latte, but that's where the similarities end. One of the biggest differences is the weight of the drink; if you pick up a latte and a cappuccino in the same size cup, the cappuccino should be significantly lighter in weight.

Traditionally, cappuccinos are truly decadent drinks that are made with either whole milk or heavy cream. However, you can make yours with any type of milk you prefer, so you don't have to feel limited by this unless you just want to have a more authentic experience. The key to a true cappuccino is to have plenty of milk foam, which is what sets it apart from any other espresso-based beverage. You are looking to create micro-foam on top of the steamed milk, which will sit lightly on top of the liquid in your cup and give you a frothy, delicious experience.

Cappuccinos are made with a double shot base, so you'll need to pull two shots of espresso to get started on this drink. If you have a smaller espresso machine that can only manage one shot at a time, just pull them back to back as quickly as you can so they do not go stale before you're able to enjoy them.

Pour the double shot of espresso into an appropriately sized mug.

Place four ounces of milk in your steaming pitcher and prepare your steaming wand. Place the steaming wand into the milk just a little away from the bottom of the pitcher and begin steaming.

Almost immediately, pull the wand back to just under the surface of the milk and steam until you have enough foam to double the milk in the pitcher. You are looking for smaller microbubbles in this foam, but if you have a few larger bubbles that's okay.

Use a spoon to gently scoop all the foam off the top of the milk and place it in the cup on top of the double shot. It should be light enough to sit on top of the drink and should not collapse immediately.

For a true, traditional cappuccino, you will not need to add any additional milk. The foam will begin to melt somewhat into the espresso and will create the perfect balance.

A real cappuccino also does not include any sugar or flavor. Of course, you can add flavor to the espresso shots if you want to, but it won't be a traditional take on the drink if you do so. If you choose to add flavor, use liquid syrup or liquid cane sugar and add a small amount to the double espresso shot before you spoon on the steamed milk.

MACCHIATOS

A somewhat lesser-known but still quite popular take on espresso is the macchiato. Like the cappuccino, the American take on this classic is very different from the original. A true Italian espresso macchiato is made with either one or two shots of espresso topped with a small amount of steamed milk. There's nothing else added to it, and sweetening it is not considered an option if you're making a traditional version of the drink. This is a good choice for anyone who enjoys very bold and somewhat bitter espresso drinks and needs a quick pick-me-up with a little caffeine. Another name for this drink is a caffe macchiato.

The American version of a macchiato is very different. This twist on the classic basically flips the traditional drink upside-down and changes the layering. It's also considered fine and even recommended to sweeten or flavor an American-style macchiato. Since the two versions are so vastly different from each other, we will give you instructions for how to make both styles of macchiato below. This way, you'll be able to try both for yourself and see which one you prefer—and how much of an espresso purist you may really be.

TO MAKE A TRADITIONAL ESPRESSO MACCHIATO:

- » Pull one or two shots of espresso into a small espresso mug or cup. Some recommend using affogato, or short, espresso shots to make the coffee naturally sweeter, but others do not. This choice is up to you.

- » Steam a small amount of milk in your steaming pitcher. Use 2% or whole milk for a traditional option or stick to other favorites if you prefer.

- » Spoon a small amount of milk onto the espresso shots in your cup. Aim for a two-to-one ratio with more espresso than milk. Do not sweeten or flavor.

TO MAKE AN AMERICAN MACCHIATO:

- » Begin by pulling two shots of espresso and setting them aside.

- » Steam enough milk to fill your cup or mug of choice. Aim for a good amount of foam on top, but don't go all the way to cappuccino levels of foam.

- » If you're going to sweeten or flavor the drink, put the syrup or sweetener into the bottom of your mug first.

- » Pour the milk and foam into the mug.

- » Carefully pour both shots of espresso on top of the milk foam. It will not be visible right on top, but you will see two "dots" of espresso where you poured it in. This is the look you're going for.

How to Make Latte Art

Have you ever been to a café where the barista has drawn a perfect heart, butterfly, or pair of wings in your coffee? Have you ever seen intricate latte art designs in photos online? If you've ever noticed latte art and caught yourself wishing you knew how to do it? Don't worry. It's not too hard to get the hang of making latte designs, and once you understand how to put together a traditional latte the right way, you're already halfway there. In this chapter, we'll give you the tips you need to know in order to make a beautiful latte topped with art.

WHAT YOU NEED

You don't need very much to get started working on your latte art magic. As long as you have access to the right ingredients and to a machine that can pull espresso shots and create steamed milk, you'll be ready to get started diving into the creative process in no time. Take some time to practice making a latte without art first and you'll be even better prepared to make beautiful designs in no time.

ESPRESSO. You cannot really make latte art without starting with espresso, as traditional coffee simply won't hold up to it.

STEAMED MILK. Ideally, you will have steamed milk from a steaming wand, but you can also make it on the stove if you have experience doing so without burning it. Whole milk, cream, and 2% make better latte art than others, but you can use any milk you prefer.

USE LARGE, WIDE MUGS. You need something big enough to hold the drink while giving you plenty of room to create and design.

TOOTHPICKS, CHOPSTICKS, OR ANYTHING ELSE SIMILARLY SHAPED. These instruments will help you gently move the milk around as needed in the cup to create the art you're looking for. Try to use wooden items so you don't disrupt the flavor of the espresso with plastic or metal.

PRACTICE. Nobody gets it right the first time, so be patient with yourself as you learn. You may need to make quite a few lattes before you get the hang of your latte art, so have some fun with it!

Remember to pour quickly enough to keep the milk moving the way it needs to, but not so fast that you splash it or the espresso.

Keep the pitcher of milk close to the top of the drink when pouring, but not so close that the pitcher scrapes the foam.

EASY DESIGNS TO TRY AT HOME

Here are a few simple latte art designs you can try for yourself. Of course, there are many more complicated styles you may want to delve into after you learn how to do these, but it's a good idea to start small and work your way up. Although latte art isn't too challenging, there is a knack to it, and it takes a little time to learn. Remember that only espresso and steamed milk can be used to make latte art.

HEART. The classic latte art design, the heart, is one of the easiest to master. Start pouring milk back and forth to make a large circle in the center of the drink. Then, pull the milk quickly forward to create a straight line that divides the heart shape at the top and makes the point at the bottom. This quick motion can be tricky, so try it until you get it right.

Another simple twist on the heart design involves making many small hearts around the edge of the cup. To do this, pour a little milk near the edge of the mug and stop as soon as you notice a white spot on top. Repeat this process several times around the perimeter of the mug. Drag a toothpick or chopstick through the dots quickly to make the divide between the heart and add the points at the bottom of each one.

LEAF. This simple design is another good choice for beginners. Pour your milk slowly from side to side in the cup, creating stripes as you work your way from the top to the bottom of the mug. At the end, divide the design with a quick pour down the middle, just like with the heart design.

FLOWER. This one is a little tougher, but it's a good intermediate latte art design. Start pouring the milk down into the drink, about an inch or so from the bottom of the cup. When you're half done with this, start moving the milk from side to side, working your way across to the opposite edge of the mug. This movement can take some practice, and it's all in your wrist. Try not to overdo it by making larger motions with your arm, and you should have better control of the milk.

HELPFUL HINTS

Getting your latte art right takes time, but there are some tips and hints you can keep in mind to make the experience go a little more smoothly. Remember the following when you find yourself struggling or just want to improve your latte drawing:

Warming up your mug first with hot water (and then pouring it out) before adding the espresso can help with your latte art designs. This will help keep the espresso and milk warm and flowing more smoothly as you pour. Additionally, it's also good for improving the overall flavor and aroma of the drink.

Choose a thicker milk, like whole milk or cream, while you're learning. You can make latte art with 2%, skim, soy, and others, but it's easier to learn with heavier milks.

Master the art of steaming milk before you try latte art. You want milk that is smooth and velvety, and you need to be able to pour it without letting the foam get into your drink. A little foam is okay, but too much will affect the way the milk pours and lays in the cup, and this will make it difficult or even impossible to make latte art.

Expanding Your Horizons

Now that you've explored

everything there is to know about coffee—from farming to roasting, from brewing to building drinks—it's time to go a little beyond the norm and consider some other ways you might want to use coffee and espresso in your everyday life. Whether you're looking for a new and exciting coffee drink to try, or you want to start cooking with the flavors of espresso, we've got several suggestions below to help you get started.

COFFEE-BASED DRINKS

Coffee and espresso can be more than the traditional go-to hot drinks you know and love. Consider these options to help you find a good fit for your unique coffee needs, and don't be afraid to play around a little bit with them to create something inspired and original.

ICED COFFEE. This is one of the easiest and most common twists on regular coffee. It's simple to make, since all you need to do is cool the coffee down somewhat and pour it over ice. However, it's also easy to get the proportions wrong. As the ice in the coffee melts, it will water down the drink and can actually make it taste rather unpleasant. For this reason, it's usually recommended to use strongly brewed coffee for icing, and some companies and vendors will offer specific blends intended for this purpose, too.

BLACK TIE. This coffee drink is also known as a Thai iced tea. This is a very powerful drink with a big caffeine punch. The drink is made by boiling water and steeping Thai tea mix with sugar for a few minutes. While the tea steeps, prepare a glass filled nearly all the way with ice. Add a tablespoon of condensed milk and a shot of espresso to the ice in the glass. Pour the steeped tea over the top and then finish it off with another two tablespoons of dairy—either whole milk or cream for best results. Stir until the entire drink is blended together well.

CHAI TEA LATTE. A chai tea latte can be one of many things, but they are all very similar. In some instances, people use the phrase "chai latte" to refer to a drink that is made from steeping chai tea in steamed milk, with no coffee involved at all. However, technically speaking, this drink should be made with a shot of regular brewed coffee stirred in at the end to give it a distinct spicy, bitter flavor. Some cafés will use a shot of espresso instead of brewed coffee instead, and this is referred to as a "dirty chai."

RED EYE. This is another strong pick-me-up kind of drink, so named for its high caffeine content and the implication that it will prepare you for a red-eye shift or flight. This drink is simple, but it has a kick. It's made with a cup of brewed coffee—usually dark roast, but any roast is fine—with a shot of espresso poured in at the end. It's up to the drinker to determine whether or not it needs sugar or milk.

IRISH COFFEE. A true Irish coffee is a little bit more than just coffee and alcohol put together, but this is the general idea. To make an Irish coffee, first heat up a mug with hot water and then empty it out. Pour in enough hot, freshly brewed coffee to fill about three-quarters of the mug. Stir in a tablespoon of brown sugar and then add a jigger of Irish whiskey, stirring gently to disperse it throughout the drink. Finally, top it off by gently pouring heavy cream into the drink.

BLENDED COFFEE/FRAPPÉ. This type of drink may not appeal very much to a coffee purist, but the truth is that blended cold coffee beverages are very popular. These drinks are usually made by putting milk, coffee or espresso, ice, and flavorings into a blender and letting it work its magic. They have a consistency sort of like a milkshake, but not exactly. Depending on the preference of the person drinking it, these beverages can be changed and altered in all sorts of ways.

COFFEE-BASED DESSERTS

When you love the taste of coffee and can't get enough of it, you might want to try making some desserts with coffee and espresso as an ingredient, too. Try the options below for some good starters, and then expand even further to find more interesting ways to incorporate coffee into your after dinner treats.

TIRAMISU. This is the classic coffee dessert, and you may have tried it before. This decadent treat is made from ladyfingers (which are similar to sponge cake) that are soaked in coffee to give them a distinct flavor. These coffee cakes are layered between sweetened mascarpone cheese and the whole concoction is topped off with cocoa shavings. This is a very well-known and beloved dessert that has several variations, and you can easily tweak it, redesign it, and make it your own.

ESPRESSO BROWNIES. Love the taste of brownies and want to take them up a notch? Consider adding some espresso to the mix! Espresso brownies can be a delicious, rich, and indulgent way to get your coffee and chocolate fix at the same time. It's easy to change the recipe for most brownies to incorporate espresso, but you can also find specific recipes intended for this purpose as well.

Mocha truffles. Mocha truffles are chocolate truffles that have either espresso or coffee as an ingredient. Using a coffee element for your truffle filling can give the candies a distinct flavor and aroma that adds layers of interest to the dessert, rather than relying solely on chocolate.

Coffee mousse. Last but not least, consider making a coffee mousse if you want something light and airy but still packed with coffee taste. You can make a coffee mousse by sprinkling gelatin over cold coffee and folding whipped cream and beaten egg whites into it. This is the same concept as making other types of mousse, but it utilizes coffee as the liquid component.

Conclusion

The world of coffee is a vibrant and exciting one. Understanding the whole coffee experience can help you enjoy the drink in ways you never have before. Knowing how to buy and choose coffee, as well as where it comes from and what it takes to grow it, may improve your ability to make better purchasing decisions. And of course, learning how to make different drinks—from roasting to grinding to brewing right in your own home—can allow you to create beverages you'll want to sip over and over again. Now that you have expanded your knowledge of this classic drink, you can share your coffee passion with your family and friends!

FROM A GREAT DREAM TO GRAND OPENING:

HOW TO START YOUR VERY OWN *Coffee Shop*

STELLA PERRY

Introduction

There's something magical about a coffee shop. The warm, steamy aroma of roasted coffee beans and dripping espresso. The tasty treats that await inside glass cases. The shine of early morning light off the steel machinery. The bustling clink of ceramic mugs and plates that awakens the senses. That personal experience when the barista calls your name. And of course, that deep sense of satisfaction when the delicious beverage you've been craving is finally in your hand. Whether you're starting your day or grabbing an afternoon pick-me-up, very few of us take for granted the comfort of a friendly shop that has exactly what you want, exactly when you need it.

Many of us have very fond memories attached to coffee shops. Waiting out the rain with a steaming mug of a house blend. Working on a résumé for the hundredth time in search of the perfect job opportunity with a cup of tea bought with pocket change. Meeting with friends to catch up after far too long and giggling over lattes. That blind date with that one person who was actually worthy of a second date ... and lingering over an ambitiously large mocha. The first time you heard a local musician perform that song you love. The first time you stood up and read your poetry aloud to someone that wasn't your best friend. Coffee shops tend to be multi-functional places where we can revel in our thoughts, have meaningful social interactions, or just grab a cup of delicious caffeine on our way to our next destination in an overworked day.

Some of us are so deeply moved and inspired by these feelings and memories, we feel called to open our own coffee shop. It may seem a vague process at first. You purchase a good and worthy space, put some equipment in it, brew some coffee, and then there's a coffee shop, right? Well, those are all important steps, but the process of actually planning and opening a coffee shop requires a lot of thought, a lot of preparation, and an eye toward long-term success.

If you are willing to put in the hard work and dedicated to seeing every step all the way through, you will be able to open the doors to your coffee shop. All told, the process may take many months, or even years, as you accumulate all of the funding, fixtures, and furnishings for your coffee shop. We'll take a look at what to consider when trying to find the perfect location for your coffee shop, too. It is absolutely crucial that you are not in a rush to make things happen because some steps might take longer. There will be unexpected delays. There will be frustrations aplenty. You may be armed with a solid vision and a creative spirit, but you will also need a generous helping of patience and good humor.

You'll discover, as you wade deeper and deeper into this project, that you are surrounded by great resources. Many times in this book, we'll encourage you to do research. While you're likely already very well acquainted with Google and YouTube, you'll want to dive deeper. Talk to your friends and family. Network with people in the coffee shop or restaurant industry. This book combines knowledge from generations of individuals with experience in every aspect of running a business, from Human Resource experts, life-long baristas, franchisees, executive chefs, business owners, coffee fanatics, and commercial decorators. As you work toward your goal of opening your own coffee shop, you will wear all of these hats—sometimes it will feel like you're wearing them all at once! Stay focused and stay true to your vision and your budget. Stay calm, and your dreams will follow you anywhere!

There are many types of coffee shops, from drive-through roadside kiosks to grand cafe experiences. Some shops serve just one or two specialties, while others serve full menus of creative beverages and a rotating menu of seasonal sandwiches and meals. There are franchise coffee shops, independent mom-and-pop coffee shops, and coffee shops that operate within a mall or shop. This book is written to help guide you through many of the things any coffee shop owner will need to consider, but your specific location and situation may hold some slightly different or additional things to bear in mind. The number one recommendation of every professional in the food industry, regardless of capacity, is to always, *always* do your research.

There will be times when you need to consult a professional. Accountants, contractors, realtors, and lawyers are just a few of the resources you may need to add to your team as you move closer and closer to Opening Day. While it may be tempting to do as much work as possible on your own, think about how you would feel if your business began blossoming, only to be shut down due to an avoidable violation. When in doubt, paying a professional a bit now can save you endless expenses and frustration down the line when something goes wrong. This is not about opening a coffee shop as quickly and cheaply as you can; this is about arming yourself to make good decisions when creating your very own business.

As you read through this book, you'll notice we have included some helpful resources to get your imagination started. This includes some tables and charts you can incorporate into your own planning portfolio, as well as some links that can help guide you to various resources to get you started on your research. None of these should be considered exhaustive, but merely an illustration of the vast number of possibilities for your venture. We aren't specifically endorsing any particular method, supplier, or resource, but rather guiding you toward finding a solution that works best for your particular coffee shop, your budget, and your needs.

You may wish to take notes. You may wish to pause at a certain point to do a little internet searching. You may want to highlight concepts to think about later. Again, take your time with this process. Business owners know a lot, and savvy business owners never stop learning. From the very first concept of your business plan brainstorm session to cutting the ribbon at the grand opening, this book is designed to stimulate the thought process to make sure you are aware of the things many people never consider when first dreaming of opening their own coffee shop.

Step 1: Creating a Business Plan

There are two very important ingredients in any thriving business: a vision and a plan. For many of us, the vision comes first and that's a great place to start! By being aware of all the elements that need to go into both the vision and the plan, you can be well on your way toward making that dream come true. First, you need to iron out all of the details.

Brainstorming the business plan is a key step in realizing both the vision and the plan. You cannot skip or skimp on this step. In fact, you will likely revisit and revise this step many times—not only while working toward Opening Day, but throughout the life of your establishment. The business plan is all about forming the requirements that will make your business run successfully.

Research is key throughout the entire process, but especially in these early days of brainstorming. Whether you have a very solid vision of what you want your shop to look like or a vague idea of the flow of things, you'll need to invest some time and thought into creating the business plan. There are quite a few things you'll need to do before you even get started.

Visit as many coffee shops as you can. Big chains. Little independent shops. Bakeries that happen to sell coffee. If there's a shop in your niche, pop in. Grab a cup of coffee and observe what makes the place run. Who is the clientele? Do they seem to be regulars, or just passing through? How many people are on staff? How does the coffee taste? What is the mood of the place? As you visit more and more shops, you'll see how different aspects make different shops tick, and as you observe these varying methods and environments, you may start picking out things you'd like to add to your plan, and things you definitely don't want in your shop.

As you're in this brainstorming stage, it's a good idea to have a notepad or tablet with you at all times. Inspiration can come anywhere and anytime. No detail is insignificant at this point, even if they conflict with each other. Your goal is to create a thriving business that reflects you and your imagination. Remember, you're going to be responsible for every single detail of this business, from the color of the cups to the volume of the ambient music.

The more thoughts you capture now, the easier it will be to whittle them down into a business plan. Eventually, as you do more and more research, these seemingly scattered thoughts and notes will start becoming cohesive. You'll start thinking in terms of "how will I do that in my shop?" You'll watch servers create frothy concoctions and wonder if your future employee will be able to match their performance. Every experience you have in a coffee shop from now on is going to be a learning experience. You may never look at a cup of coffee the same way again!

What are you going to sell?

The key ingredient of a coffee shop is, of course, coffee. But what kind of coffee? There are so many options out there. Flavored, internationally sourced, locally roasted, espresso, decaffeinated ... there are far more options these days than "regular or decaf."

Are you going to serve specialty drinks? If so, what kinds? While what you brainstorm now doesn't have to be fully committed to the menu, get a feel for what you'd like to serve. More importantly, consider how you'll serve it. For example, if you'd like to offer a mocha beverage, write out the ingredients: espresso, milk, and chocolate. What types of milk would you like to offer your customers? How about temperature? Some coffee shops offer the choice of a hot mocha, an iced mocha, or a frozen mocha. Offering these options requires the same ingredients, but also ice, a blender, and different cup options. Later, we're going to get more involved in the concept of inventory and sourcing, but none of that can be done until you have an idea of what is going to go into those cups.

Speaking of cups, what sizes will the beverages be? Not only will hot and cold drinks require different types of cups, but offering different sizes will require different stock as well. Will beverages be served differently if they are "for here" or "to go"? What about straws? Plastic straws tend to be an environmental concern, but paper straws can dissolve, and stainless steel straws can be expensive. Again, this is not the time to dive into the budget concerns—that will come soon enough—but now is when you consider the overall logistics of what goes where and how.

Once you've got a feel for how the "coffee" part of the coffee shop will look, what about non-coffee drinks? Will you offer hot tea, and if so, what kinds? What about kids' drinks, like hot chocolate or juice? What about ice water?

How about food? Will you make your own food? Will you have bakers or sandwich makers on staff, or will you bring in food from a local bakery or sandwich shop? Food can be extra tricky, because you need to consider peak times at your coffee shop, and what kind of appetite your clientele may have. At this stage, it's best to jot down a few ideas of foods and treats you would like to serve, then revisit this as plans become more clear. We'll get much more in-depth about the food process, but at this stage, you'll want to have some general ideas about your overall goals for serving tasty treats to your customers.

Try to dream up scenarios in which customers come to your coffee shop, so you can walk through what they may want. Let's say customers come into your shop on their way to work. They might want a hand-held, easy-to-eat sandwich or pastry to take with them. On the other hand, students that come to study in your space might want a snack to enjoy while they read or write. Moms stopping by for a pick-me-up while shuttling the kids from school to activities might want to grab quick snacks for the kids, as well.

Select a few options for each type of situation. For example:

Breakfast: cinnamon rolls, apple danish, bran muffins, chocolate chip muffins, bear claws
Sandwiches to go: egg and cheese, bagel and cream cheese, sausage, egg, and cheese
In-house breakfast: egg and sausage with toast, breakfast potatoes
Cookies: peanut butter, chocolate chip, frosted sugar
Snacks: crispy rice treats, granola, fresh fruit, cheese and crackers

This is not meant to be an all-inclusive list, but simply an example of some of the situations in which patrons of your coffee shop may want to grab a bite to eat in addition to their beverage. Again, the goal of this exercise is to set the parameters and bring the vision further into focus. You may ultimately scrap every menu decision you make here, but this is a great start to forming your ideas. By considering who you hope your patrons to be, you can anticipate how you can best capture their needs with your business plan, which will lead you closer to your goal of opening your coffee shop.

Where are you going to get it?

Sourcing your beverages and food items is a crucial step that can help you understand what is feasible for your business model. We'll drill down into this topic in a future chapter, but this is a good time to brainstorm places where you can get the products you want.

For example, if you really love the cinnamon rolls at the bakery down the street, you have the option to see if the bakery would be willing to work with you to supply their rolls, or you can start
searching for a recipe that accurately mimics their product. Each option

comes with its own considerations. If you're going to contract with a bakery to supply their goods, you'll have to be able to get a feel for supply and demand so you can order the correct inventory. If you're going to make them yourself, you'll have to consider purchasing all of the ingredients and having a space to make a large volume of cinnamon rolls. If that space is off-site, you'll also have to consider transporting those rolls to the coffee shop and storing them.

For each of the items you've considered serving, jot down some places where you can get what's needed to make that item. Consider local wholesale shops or stores that offer wholesale discounts. What about national suppliers? Don't worry about comparing costs at this point—this is the part of the process where you let the ideas flow. Include every possible avenue so you can have the most possible options at your fingertips.

Who is your staff?

As you consider what you're going to serve, you'll need to consider how it's going to be served. Beyond "in a cup" or "on a plate," consider how your coffee shop will be run. What roles will each staff member have?

You might want to map out the flow of how an order might be processed. For example:

Customer orders at register > cashier rings up the order and gives order to barista > barista makes and serves the drink > food is managed by a third staff member, who plates or bags the food items and hands them to the customer

Or

Customer orders at register > barista both rings up the order and begins to make the drink and food > once all food and beverages are complete, they are handed back to the customer

Each process has its pros and cons and may be more feasible at different times of the day. During peak time, having one staff member handle all of the steps might create a lag in taking and processing new orders. At the same time, this might be the perfect process during slower times of the day. To determine the best fit, you need to figure out who will be in your coffee shop, and when.

Who is your clientele?

Nearly everyone can find something to love about a coffee shop, so it's always a good idea to be warm and welcoming to anyone who might be seeking a hot beverage and a treat. At the same time, you might be interested in creating a footprint in a particular niche.

If you live in a town with a large college or university, you might be interested in catering to the students and faculty. You might consider offering student discounts and free Wi-Fi. If you want to create a welcoming place for students to work, you'll want to consider things like low-volume music, electrical outlets for laptops and other device chargers, ambient lighting for reading, and seats that are comfortable. You may also consider that a student will take up space for a longer period of time but may make fewer purchases during that time since they are focused more on their work than ordering large amounts of food and drink.

Perhaps you want to create a meeting space. In that case, you might want to offer larger tables that accommodate gatherings of people, or spaces that are more private, so these groups do not interfere with other patrons. You might want to offer share-size snacks for these groups or carafes of coffee that can be enjoyed while they meet and discuss business.

If you'd like to build a child-friendly coffee shop, you might consider having some books or activities like coloring books on hand. You can even create small "busy bags" that can be checked out from the counter that keep younger minds and hands entertained while parents take a moment out of their busy day for a comforting beverage and a little peace and quiet. You'll also want to have food and drink that are suitable for kids, like non-caffeinated beverages, and food that doesn't create a giant mess that staff will have to clean up.

Traditionally, creative types flock to coffee shops. Will you offer exhibits for local artists? Open mic night for poets, writers, singers, and musicians? Will you have live music from time to time? All of these special events can be a great draw for customers but will require additional equipment, appropriate space, and considerations for supplies and staffing. Knowing what you want to happen in your space will help you narrow down your business plan to accommodate these interesting points.

What makes your business special?

Hand-in-hand with considering clientele is deciding why customers will want to come to your coffee shop. What sets you apart from the chain shops that can be found on nearly every corner? What will make a customer prefer to stop at your shop, rather than heading through the drive-thru of a local franchise?

For many people, the environment of a coffee shop is key. Is it bright and bustling, or dim and offers privacy? Are the drinks creative and flavorful? Do you showcase local artists, musicians, and more? For some, just having super-comfortable chairs can be a huge draw, especially for students who might miss the comforts of home. Anything you do to set your coffee shop apart from any other shop is the niche that you will fill, so consider all of the research you've done. What do regulars want? What do regulars LOVE? What types of things will make people want to come to your coffee shop before any other coffee shop?

Let your own tastes and personality shine here. The more you love your concept, the more you'll be devoted to watching it flourish. If you only half-heartedly appreciate your concept, you might devote less time to making it work. There are plenty of ways you can let your own interests shine in your coffee shop without going overboard. If you love books, consider having a wall of books patrons can read while they enjoy their drinks. This will put you on the hunt for unique books to add to your collection. If you enjoy plants, perhaps your coffee shop includes a beautiful array of succulents and indoor plants that give the environment a clean, homey feel. If you are a music enthusiast, perhaps you can cultivate an amazing collection of records to play so your patrons can discover a new favorite.

These are, of course, just a few ideas as to how your coffee shop can become unique and attract clientele. This is an opportunity to express your passions, so think of things that you share and enjoy with others, then think of fun ways to share that passion with even more and more people. Be creative and jot down a few possibilities!

Review local laws and health criteria

As full disclosure, please note that this book was written with the United States market in mind, so for those outside the US, please take the time to look up both local and federal laws for your area. Compliance with laws and health codes is absolutely crucial when it comes to running a business that involves serving food and drink. In many places, health code scores are posted publicly, and a poor mark or negative review can absolutely ruin a business at any time.

When considering your concept, do research on what is and isn't acceptable due to law and health code. For example, cat cafes (and even more exotic animal-themed cafes!) are popping up everywhere, but have a very distinct code as to how animals can come in contact with the customers, and frequently require waivers for patrons who may become inadvertently harmed by the animals.

Health codes vary from state to state and can change, depending on whether food is served in-house or if you choose not to serve food at all. There are codes for sanitation, codes for storing food, codes for cleanliness, and more. Be aware of all the restrictions and regulations before committing to a concept! There are far too many rules and regulations to list here, but some helpful links to get you started have been included in the index.

At this stage, you may have tons and tons of notes regarding your own coffee shop, and if you're a bit bewildered, you've done it right. Now is the time to slowly narrow things down a bit until you have a solid concept. This may not be accomplished in one day. You may find yourself running idea after idea past a trusted friend or family member. You may wish to spread all of your notes out on a large surface and piece them together one by one like a giant puzzle, or you may want to create a digital work board of how things will work. Some people even prefer to draw out their ideas to have a visual of how things will flow. Whatever your preferred method is, be sure to have all of your digital files clearly labeled, and all of your physical documents neatly stored. This process is going to be chaotic enough without trying to find that one specific note that you thought you put here, over and over again.

Take your time at this point. Don't rush ahead to get started without knowing exactly what you're looking to start. Really research drink recipes—we've included a few examples in the index to get the creative java juices flowing—and consider what you want to serve. Dive deep into your community to figure out who your customers are going to be, as well as what kind of space will best serve them. And most importantly, create a plan that you can feel committed to and passionate about, and ready to invest in fully.

A Note About the Next Steps - A Brief Pep Talk

Your business plan has now officially begun, but you're far from done at this point. In this first step, you have created the master plan upon which all of the next steps will rely. As you proceed, your plan will very likely change. Be flexible. Keep a focus on what you really want to accomplish with your coffee shop, but acknowledge that reality is what it is. You will encounter many setbacks along the way, and sometimes it will feel as if things are "too easy." The reason we establish these plans so early in the process is because they can always be revisited and changed.

Before you continue, really stop and think about how you're going to define success. Will you be happy when you open the doors on any old coffee shop, or will you not rest until the marble countertops match the swatch you've saved for years? There's no wrong answer here, but compromise is very, very important when building your business. As we proceed, you'll establish an overall budget, you'll find the right location, and we'll go shopping for all of the items you need to open your very own coffee shop. Start with big dreams, but be careful that you don't get swept away with extravagances, or start too small to sustain your business. Regardless of where your vision and plan start and end, the ultimate goal is to create a profitable business that reflects your ideal coffee shop.

Step 2: Do the Math

In the first step, we carefully created a business plan by jotting down all of the ideas and thoughts and considerations for your future business and carefully considering all your ideas into a plan that just might work. You have taken the time to do research and learned what makes similar businesses in your area thrive. By brainstorming every possible detail, you have taken the opportunity to consider a lot of options before settling on the one that speaks most to your vision and plan.

The goal of the first step was to create the overall blueprint to follow as you strive toward the grand opening of your very own coffee shop, but it's important that you do not discard all of your notes just yet! In this step, we'll be putting together the financial considerations of your new enterprise. Bear in mind that this step is about finding out what you can afford, and how to afford it. As the numbers tally up, you may find that some dreams are a bit out of your budget for now and having alternative options at hand can be helpful to keep you pressing forward toward fulfilling your dreams, rather than reaching a stalling point.

What tools and resources will you need to help you?

For many new business owners, this is a good time to consider hiring an accountant. While coming up with the figures you can afford is something you may feel comfortable doing yourself, a professional can help you take into consideration any taxes or fees that might be required in your area. A professional accountant can also help you organize all of your receipts, paperwork, and deeds to ensure you're prepared for every financial consideration, too.

Depending on your own abilities with keeping track of expenses and income, you may feel comfortable consulting with the accountant at the start of business and come tax time. There are many software options that are also available for business owners, and once you are set straight on the path of keeping records with professional help, you may be perfectly comfortable sorting all these records yourself. We've included a few examples of these types of software in the index, but ask yourself these important questions when choosing an option that fits your comfort level and business:

1. How comfortable are you with bookkeeping? Be honest with yourself. While the software will do the math for you, it will only be as good as the person entering figures. Take into consideration your financial literacy to ensure that the software you choose is something you can comfortably work with every single day.

2. Do plenty of research. There are specific types of software for small cafes and shops that might suit your anticipated business needs. Take a look at what features each option offers. Do you need a cloud-based program, which you can operate from any computer or device, anywhere? Do you need a program that offers 24-hour support? Do you want your bookkeeping software to include payroll functionality?

3. What about budget? Most software programs have a monthly cost associated with them, so when considering your monthly expenses, don't forget to include your bookkeeping software!

4. Data security considerations must be addressed, as well. How does this particular software back up and provide security for the data that you enter?

Keeping each of these questions in mind will help you as you discover and analyze the different types of bookkeeping software available to you. Be sure to be honest with yourself at every step—while it may seem easy to keep track of taxes for a small workforce, what happens when your staff grows? What if the taxation regulations change in your area? Will you be able to teach another partner how to use this software, in the event that you need to step away for a day off? Discuss these concerns with your accountant, if you're unsure of how to answer these questions on your own.

Now, let's consider the actual expenses that would be associated with the actual start-up of your coffee shop. Your goal will be to create a table that outlines each expense as a line item. This will not only help you stay organized for your own benefit, but many financiers require detailed business plans with these figures, as well. At this point, though, the goal is to get a general idea of what you might need. Instead of line items, you might have general categories at this point. For now, leave the "cost" section blank. Take this process step-by-step so you can truly consider where you want—and need—your hard-earned money to go to create the best profit. You'll revisit this table many times as we walk through all the considerations of opening your coffee shop. Line items may change over time, and you might be surprised by some of the dollar amounts you enter in the cost section, but creating a simple chart like this will help you stay organized and aware of your budget at all times.

Your first version of this table might look a bit like this. As you get closer and closer to Opening Day, you'll move further away from estimating the cost per category of expenses, and have an actual to-the-penny figure for individual line items. Remember: this is a process that starts big and becomes more and more refined as you get closer to your goal.

First Month's Lease and Security Deposit/ Down Payment and Mortgage

Insurance

Inspection Fees (health inspection, OSHA, HVAC, etc) and Code Prep

Utility Connection Fees and Deposits (water, electric, gas, trash removal, recycling, etc)

Business License and Legal

Office equipment: Register, POS system, receipt printer, order ticket printer (if necessary), credit card reader, printer paper, pens/notebooks, computer for bookkeeping

Coffee Equipment: Espresso Machine, Coffee Makers, Coffee Pots, Carafes, Bean Grinders, Espresso Cups and Filters, Milk Pitchers, Hot Water Steaming Equipment, Thermometers

Other Appliances: Oven, Refrigerator, Freezer, Icemaker, Cold Case, Display Case, Toaster, Microwave, Blenders, Prep Sinks, Dishwasher, Bathroom Equipment (if not included in the space)

Serving Equipment: Cups, Saucers, Plates, Utensils, Tongs, Spatulas

Paper Goods: Wrappers, Napkins, To Go Cups (hot and cold), Lids (hot and cold), Stir Sticks, Cup Sleeves, Straws, Toilet Paper, Paper Towels

Cleaning Supplies: Disinfectant per local procedure for all dishes, surfaces, restrooms, tables, floors, etc., Mops, Buckets, Brooms, Dustpans, Cloths for cleaning spills, Supplies for keeping windows clean

Uniforms for staff

Furniture: Chairs, tables, service counters, counters on which to place machinery, trash bins, storage and shelving

Labor/Staffing

Product: Coffee, syrups, milk, all per the recipes you finalize

Decor: painting the walls, finishing the floor, light fixtures, sound system, security system (if not supplied by space)

This list is, of course, just an example of some of the things you may or may not need to open your own coffee shop. Modify your chart for your own business; for example, if you do not plan to serve any type of food, you will not need things like a toaster, an oven, or plates. You may choose not to have a display case or cold case for grab-and-go items. Regardless of the items that actually fill your list, make sure you've considered every aspect of daily business. This list will be your guide for each following step of the process, from finding a location and space to fit your needs to determining supply chain, to shopping for the bits and pieces that bring your business's ambiance to life.

How are you going to pay for it all?

Now that you have an idea of what you're going to need to bring this dream to life, it's time to consider where the money is going to come from. You may have your own savings to put toward start-up, but as you dive into the details, you may start to realize that perhaps a little bit more is needed to provide ample padding for all of the "what ifs" that you most assuredly will encounter.

Let's start with your own savings. What do you have in your own bank account? Keep in mind, the world will not stand still while you focus on opening your coffee shop. You'll still need to pay your monthly bills, so set aside your active budget and don't touch it. Getting financing down the line on any rental space, equipment, and more will be deeply impaired if you default on any of your existing expenses. Keep your own financial record as clean as possible to ensure you have the capacity and options available for any financial assistance you may need throughout the process.

Putting aside the funds that you will need for your personal expenses, as well as a buffer for your own emergency needs, consider what part of your overall savings you're willing to commit to your new business. The temptation to cash out all of your retirement funds or investments may be high, but keep in mind that doing so may have tax implications, as well as depleting your nest egg. This is another part of the process in which having a professional accountant on hand will help mitigate any accidental financial mishaps you may make without realizing it!

Next, consider what you want to have in hand as start-up capital. While we haven't assigned prices to all of the items you'll need in order to open your doors, consider how much you can feasibly have available before you get started.

Something Borrowed

One option is to pursue a loan. There are many, many loans available for small business owners, so it is absolutely essential to do a considerable amount of research here. Your bank or financial institution may have loan options available. The Small Business Association is another potential source for a loan, as well. Companies like Swift Capital specialize in fast, online loans for small business owners.

As you do your research, you'll see a lot of unfamiliar terms that may make your head swirl. Since you're going into this venture as a new business owner, you're going to need to choose a loan program that makes sense while you wait to collect on profit. In addition to your regular expenses, and the expenses of running a business, you will need to pay the loan back as well, so be careful when reading all of the terms and conditions. You may be interested in one or more of the following options:

- A small business line of credit, which will provide a certain amount of funds, upon which you can draw credit with a monthly interest rate.
- Working capital loans can be very short-term loans to help a business owner have the funds on hand to deal with day-to-day expenses in times where profit can be uncertain.
- Term loans are a frequently chosen option for start-ups, as they come with a set dollar amount, and generally a fixed interest rate.
- Equipment loans are, as the name suggests, strictly for the purchase of equipment, and typically require a 20% down payment. These are generally secured through an equipment vendor, but may be sought elsewhere.
- Small business credit cards. Like the credit card you may carry in your wallet each day, there are both pros and cons of pursuing this option. You'll be able to easily track business expenses by applying them to this card alone, but interest rates could get out of hand if payments aren't made promptly and in full.

Another option for pursuing funding is to engage a partner or a group of investors. These are people, groups, and services that are willing to provide funding either with or without a cost to you. Some of these may seem too good to be true, in which case they probably are. There are still many reputable lending programs that can aid you in start-up capital for your coffee shop.

- Online lending platforms: Prosper, TrustLeaf, OnDeck, and Lending Club.
- Personal marketing: You may have friends or family members who are willing to gift you some cash to get started. There may be others in your circle who are willing to join you in your venture. Some people say it's best to avoid doing business with friends and family; however, there are generations of family-run businesses that say otherwise. Only you will be able to evaluate the relationship you have with potential investors within your circle, and how much control they wish to exercise over your business.
- Incubators and accelerators: These businesses help make your dreams of owning a business a reality. Not only do these groups offer potential investors, but also mentors, networking opportunities, and solid expertise. The National Business Incubation Association offers a directory of options that can help you find resources in your state, as well as local economic development services, and locations of Small Business Association resources in your area.
- Angel Networks: Angel Networks seem heaven-sent. These groups provide investors who can provide guidance and mentorship through the early processes of starting your business. This is a fantastic way to connect those who wish to inspire future business leaders in your niche with those, like you, who are wading into the unfamiliar waters of starting your very first enterprise.

Making New Friends and Investors

Another option, which is very popular in this social day and age, is crowdfunding. There are several websites that allow you to request funds from interested parties, such as Kickstarter, Peerbackers, OurCrowd, and Indiegogo. Each site has its own typical audience, and your intention to raise funds for your coffee shop can be broadcast in various ways, such as email, newsletter, and social media. Social media is, of course, an excellent choice for spreading the word, as each person who sees the post has the option of sharing the post with others. While crowdfunding typically raises donations in smaller amounts, it often garners a great deal of attention, helping you market your brand and bring your coffee shop into the limelight before the doors even open!

One source of crowdfunding that can be lots of fun is the old-fashioned method of getting out in the public. Announce your intentions to the community. Participate in community events on behalf of your business. For example, if your community has a flea market or craft event, team up with vendors to raise funds toward the opening of your shop. In fact, if you're handy, or have friends willing to donate to the cause, you could become a vendor yourself! Show up on behalf of your brand at places where the community gathers, be it street fairs, art fairs, or cultural events, and get the local folks excited about the new business that will soon be on their doorsteps. You may need to print some logo items or have samples available, but that level of investment will be small, compared to the potential funds that could head your way from excited investors and future customers. In fact, if you plan to provide space for local groups to meet, artists to exhibit, or musicians to perform, this is a great place to start networking with them.

At this stage, you've got some rudimentary plans for gaining the funding you need to proceed with the next steps. Often, you'll need to have a very solid business plan in place before applying for a loan of any kind, so the steps going forward from here will often lead back to the first step of creating a business plan, and this step of gaining the financial security to start shopping. Planning a business of any kind tends to be less linear and more circular, but if you start investigating financial options now, you'll have a better idea of your actual budget as you proceed with finding your shop and filling it with everything you'll need to make your coffee shop a success.

Step 3: Create the Space

Having a solid business plan is a requirement, and having a budget is crucial, but there's one really important element that will help bring this whole dream together: a space!

Many people want to choose the space before the first two steps, but there are a few important reasons to resist this urge. First, you need to know what the overall business will look like in order to know what type of space you need. This is why we drew up the business plan first. Perhaps, after looking at all your ideas and dreams, you discovered that a kiosk type of space would be absolutely perfect for your coffee shop. Alternately, you might realize you want to open a bakery in conjunction with your coffee shop, which requires space (and budget) for ovens and serving. In working with potential investors and mentors, perhaps you realized a few things about the capacity of your start-up, or in working within the community, you learned that there was an appetite amongst your peers for a totally different type of space than you initially envisioned.

As the pieces of the puzzle come together, you may find yourself revisiting and revamping your business plan over and over. The final business plan, which you may submit to receive financial backing, may look very different from your original daydreams, and while that may seem frustrating, it's generally a good thing. Your final business plan should reflect an operation that can financially sustain itself and bring benefits to the community. Success should not be measured by whether you get the perfect wall sconces, but whether your coffee shop is appreciated by its customers and brings in a profit over time. Keep this in mind as you start looking for the perfect spot for your coffee shop.

Renting Vs. Buying

Your very first consideration should be whether you wish to buy your location or lease. There are, of course, pros and cons to each decision. If you don't have the capital to purchase the location, then this option is off the table immediately, and leasing wins this round, but there are some things to keep in mind when considering each option.

When leasing, it needs to be clearly established what the property owner does and does not permit, as far as any upgrades or remodelling of the property. If the property owner won't let you make the adjustments that might be required to bring the property up to code, it won't work out. This is why we took the time to research laws and regulations when creating a business plan. You should be largely aware of what is required to make your business legal, and discuss these needs with the property owner before settling into a contract.

It's also very important that both the landlord and you agree on who is responsible for what. This can include everything from maintenance issues (what happens if the HVAC system quits and the business has to close for a few days?) to repair of the property (who makes sure the parking lot is paved?), to liability issues (who is considered liable if a tree falls on a customer's car during a wind storm?), to seasonal maintenance (who is responsible for snow removal?). A lot of these issues boil down to insurance agreements, which we'll discuss shortly, but very frequently, a landlord may cover these types of issues in the rental agreement, especially in the case of areas that may be shared between several businesses, like parking lots or HVAC systems.

You also need to examine the terms of the lease. What happens if the business does not succeed? We're obviously working toward putting our best foot forward and gaining profit, but unexpected things can happen that are far, far out of our control. What happens to the lease if you have to abruptly pull the plug on the coffee shop at any time? What happens to the contents of the building—do you have a set amount of time to remove your property? How much notice does the landlord require? It is generally in the landlord's best interest to have that spot occupied, so there may be an escape clause of sorts, but you might be charged a fee. It is always best to know these things ahead of time to avoid unpleasant surprises or visits from debt collectors.

What about buying? Generally speaking, buying a spot isn't within the budget or project scope for a first-time entrepreneur, but there are always exceptions to every rule. If you have experience with property management, buying a space might be a long-term investment that goes beyond this coffee shop plan. Business may go incredibly well, and you'll wish to expand in a few years, in which case you can lease out the original space to new tenants.

As the owner, you control everything. You can create your dream property, whether through remodeling or building from the ground up. You can control every inch of electric wiring, every screw and nail, and every inch of paint. Yes, that is going to require more money. Yes, that is going to require more time. However, having this level of control means your rent will never change. You will never have to argue with the property owner over who should take care of what. Furthermore, you can manage this property for the rest of your life.

At the same time, owning the space means you are responsible for absolutely everything. Every expense. Every insurance claim. Every legal requirement. Every zoning consideration. Just like with a house, any time anything goes wrong, it is automatically your responsibility. Are you prepared for that level of financial commitment?

The Search for the Perfect Spot

Once you've decided whether to lease or buy your space, you'll be able to start the search. You've probably begun a few preliminary internet searches for the perfect space for your coffee shop. It's always a good idea to look and to keep looking. While you may feel pressured to take the first space that might "kinda sorta" work, it is very important to remember that this shop is going to be your investment, and it won't work just because you want it to work. Having many options to review will help you understand what criteria you really need to make your business plan work. You may feel that having a lot of options will cloud your judgment or make the selection process more difficult, but consider each option a learning experience.

When you enter "coffee shop for sale" or "coffee shop for rent" in Google, you'll probably find thousands of results, some of which may not be entirely relevant. You may want to be more specific, such as "coffee shop for sale in TOWN" or "restaurant space for rent in TOWN." You may want the assistance of a professional and look for a "commercial real estate agent in TOWN," in order to find agents who assist people like you in finding their perfect space.

Each day, try a different type of search and make note of the results. There will be some spaces that very obviously will not work, and you can dismiss those right away. The rest of the spaces will likely fall under three categories: Maybe, Good Fit, and Dream. "Maybes" will be spaces that don't immediately make your heart flutter, but that check off most of the things you need for your coffee shop to open. "Good Fits" will be in the right price range, the right location, and have generally what you need to get started. "Dream" spaces will be those that maybe you can't afford right now, or might be bigger than what you need, or might require some additional permits that you're not sure you have the patience for right now, but would otherwise be ideal.

Location Concerns

For each space that makes it to the Maybe, Good Fit, and Dream list, conduct a drive-by. In fact, conduct a drive-by, park, and walk up. Finding a space for your coffee shop isn't just about finding the prettiest storefront. As anyone with real estate experience will tell you, the most important thing is LOCATION, LOCATION, LOCATION!

Your coffee shop has to allow people to visit it. That means that the location has to be convenient for your customers. If customers have to take several one-way streets to find your shop in an alley, it is highly unlikely they'll want to detour from their daily commute just for a quick cup of coffee. At the same time, if your shop is located on an extremely busy roadway with considerable traffic, customers may be anxious to just get through all the congestion and get to work already, making them less likely to stop. Additionally, your coffee shop should be easy to find from the road. The signage and entrance should be obvious enough that even morning, bleary-eyed, pre-caffeinated drivers can easily spot it and turn in.

Once they've arrived, customers need to be able to approach the building. It may seem obvious, but consider who your clientele will be, and where they'll be coming from, as decided in your business plan. Does this space have access to abundant parking? Can local customers walk to this space? Where will the deliveries of products and supplies be made? If you plan to host events, where will people be able to unload? All of these functions must allow for the flow of traffic on the street, and not block a shared parking lot if one exists. Customers should be able to enter, park, and leave easily without becoming frustrated or having a traffic mishap. If you plan to have a drive-thru window, the flow of this traffic needs to be considered, as well.

Accessibility is another concern. The Americans with Disability Act has a variety of requirements for restaurants and coffee shops, which were part of the legal review in Step 1. Not only do these requirements impact the inside of the coffee shop, but the parking lot and entrance, as well. If you are leasing a property, this may be something the property owner has already considered, but it's always good to make sure the entire facility is compliant before you get into a situation that could negatively impact your business!

Finding the Perfect Price Point

In Step 2, we started budget considerations and outlined all of the things that will be needed before the doors open. You may have hired an accountant to help you with all of the ins and outs along the way. You may have secured—or are in the process of securing—loans for your business. This is the stage where you need to consider your budget for your space.

There are two schools of thought on this topic. Some restaurateurs believe you should at least have a preliminary budget on everything before signing a lease because you'll then have a solid plan on every point. Others believe you should find a location first, based on clientele and local appetite, and then adjust expenditures to fit the business model afterward. In actual practice, there is rarely a perfect chronological order to everything. Most loans require documentation of every expense before the money is granted, but it's impossible to know what you can afford until you know what kind of funding you have. It may all seem a circuitous catch-22 of impossibility, but there is one thing you can do to mitigate all of the questions and budgetary concerns: keep researching.

When you search for property, you will likely find listings that include the following:

- Exterior pictures
- Interior pictures
- Address

- Unit number and floor, if applicable
- Square footage
- Existing fixtures (such as kitchen, storage, natural light, street walk-up, restrooms)
- Price per square foot, per year
- Operating expenses

Because commercial spaces are often reconfigured and remodeled, the price is calculated as price per square foot, per year. If a space is advertised as 6000 square feet, and the owner is asking $10 per square foot, per year, the annual rate would be 6000 x 10 = $60,000.

Operating expenses include the costs associated with running a business from that location. Depending on your lease, this may be in addition to rent, or part of the rental price. Unfortunately, operating expenses can become very complicated and involve things outside of your control, such as building occupancy, reconciliation billing, and unexpected jumps when business in the building waxes and wanes. Always inspect the terms and conditions of the operating expenses and ask questions about how it is calculated when looking at a property and discussing with the property owner.

Another consideration that impacts both your budget and the space you choose is profit. This may not seem like an obvious conclusion but consider the entire sales process. Let's look at a coffee kiosk, to start. Drive through only. One by one, cars place their order at the speaker and receive their delicious coffee and snacks at the window. The process is efficient, and depending on staffing and machinery, you can serve X number of people per hour. Then let's consider a coffee shop where patrons are encouraged to come in and stick around. They'll need places to sit, as well as a designated place to queue. The space behind the counter has to allow for an efficient flow of business. You'll need plenty of room for baristas to correctly prepare orders as quickly as possible to prevent the flow of customers from creating a traffic jam inside the shop, in the doorway, or in the parking lot. Efficiency and profit go hand-in-hand, and the space you choose must be able to handle the flow of business.

Asking All the Right Questions

Once you've settled all of the location and financial aspects, you'll have your lists narrowed down to some possibilities that make sense on all ends. Now is the time to start following up on those leads! For each one, reach out to the listing agent or party arranging the lease or sale. Be forthright and honest and explain your purpose. They may know of reasons the property might not work well for your coffee shop and will disclose those before you get too invested in the process. They may also know of properties you might not have considered or even be aware of yet, which could equally suit your needs.

Schedule a time to meet with the listing agent or property owner. Come prepared with a list of questions, including the following (some of which may depend on whether you intend to rent or purchase):

1. How long is the standard lease? What is the exact move-in day and exact final date of the lease (unless extended)? If the space is currently occupied, what happens if they aren't out by the exact move-in day?
2. How much is rent or selling price, and what is included? Real estate taxes, operational costs, building maintenance, insurance?
3. When does rent increase, and by how much? While the property owner might not have a set schedule, they should have historical information that demonstrates rent changes in the past.
4. As discussed earlier, what kind of "escape clause" is available, in case something unforeseen should cause you to close the doors? Is subleasing an option?
5. What are the renewal procedures?

6. Can the landlord sell the property during your lease, and if so, what happens to you?
7. What are the insurance requirements for the property?
8. What are the zoning restrictions or provisions for the property?
9. Who are the neighbors? While the location may be prime, it's best to not have a direct competitor right next door. Similarly, you want to be surrounded by businesses that complement or add business to yours, and vice-versa.
10. What about CAM? CAM stands for "common area maintenance" and includes the areas you might share with other businesses, like parking lots, sidewalks, and more.

These are, of course, just a few questions to get you started. You may have additional questions once you get involved in conversation with the agent or landlord, and it's always important to ask questions as they come to mind. Asking now will prevent an ill-fated discovery down the road.

Making "Cents" of Your Space

The next step is viewing the property. If you've done your homework, you've already seen the outside and evaluated the positive and negative aspects of the storefront, parking lot, and overall visibility and access from the road. Now is the time to see what's inside.

Walk through the space at least three times. First, walk through with no expectations—just notice all of the details. What's the natural light like? Where are the vents, speakers, electric sockets? What is the feel of the interior? Are there any fixtures already in place? Where are the restrooms? Is there plumbing and gas jets in place for adding kitchen fixtures?

Next, experience the space in terms of how you want to set it up. Where is the most logical place to put the cash register? The service counter? The espresso machines? Where will the kitchen go? What lighting would be needed to improve visibility? How many tables and chairs can you fit in the space? Is there room for some of the optional features you may have considered, like a bookcase, or a performance area? Take your time with this step. Take measurements, because you'll want to block off space later when creating the final floor plan. It's absolutely critical that the space fits the business, so really consider how things will fit without creating a fire hazard or causing a traffic jam during peak business hours.

Once you've got an idea of where you want to put all of the fixtures, walk through again as if you are a customer. When you walk through the door, what will the customer see? Where does the natural traffic flow direct them? Will they become confused when looking for the restroom? Will there be enough room to wait comfortably for a drink to be prepared? Where do you naturally look to see a menu? Can a menu be placed in that location? Do you have to wander through the restaurant and seating area to form a queue? You may have to revisit these two steps a few times. While you don't want to jeopardize the time of the agent or property owner allowing you this time in their space, take notes, measurements, and pictures so you can reference this location later, if it looks promising.

Once you take this information home, you'll have the ability to create floor plans. This will be the true test to determine if this space will really work. What size and shape will the countertops be? Is there plenty of room for workers behind the counter? Are there any awkward spaces? What can you do to reduce empty space?

You may wish to pull out the graph paper and a pencil, or for a more modern take on designing a floor plan, consider one of the many apps or software options available. These programs allow you to input the dimensions of everything you may need to get a floor plan started. Even better, they often have both mobile and laptop compatibility, meaning you can access your plans anywhere. Consider what fixtures are there, if any. If you are building your own coffee shop from the ground, this obviously won't be applicable, but for those who are purchasing or leasing an existing spot, think about these things:

- What kind of counter space exists?
- What kind of storage exists?
- Are there appliances, or outlets/areas for appliances?
- Are there closets?
- Where are the doors, and do they open inward or outward?
- What about plumbing or sinks? Are they installed, or is there a designated space where these things can be added?

Regardless of whether you are leasing or purchasing a space, you may encounter a fully empty space or the remains of a previous business. If you are leasing, check what kind of allowances and restrictions they allow for adding your own fixtures. What materials can you use? What building permits will you need? Are there any limits or requirements for contractors? These are factors that will impact your budgeting, so this is a very important time to consider what additions or remodeling will be needed.

Looking Out

While the interior is the most important feature of your coffee shop, the exterior is also a significant part of the package. Will you have room for outdoor seating? What does the landscaping look like? If you're leasing, will you have any responsibilities for the landscaping?

What about signage? Much of the size and type of sign you hang to advertise your business depends on local restrictions and regulations; however, take a look at where the sign is in relation to the road. For example, think of many fast-food restaurants, which have large, glowing signs that hover above the roadways, often with marquees that display current specials. If you're looking at a property in a shopping plaza-type setting, is there a directory sign at the entrance, as well as personalized signage near the shop door? Some property owners have requirements on fonts, sizes, and colors involved in signage, so double-check this now to avoid spending money on signs you won't be able to hang.

Depending on the area, you may also want to consider security and privacy gates to protect your glass, your belongings, and your overall business when you're closed. Does the building include—or even permit—these items?

Make Sure It's on the Up-And-Up

As this process develops, you will become intimately familiar with all the legal requirements of zoning, the ADA, the health code, fire code, and all the local requirements and permits that allow you to open your coffee shop. There will be many inspections, and many codes to follow. How will this space stack up to all of these regulations? The property owner or agent may have some details, especially if the space has been used for a similar business in the past, but doing your research is essential to make sure you don't miss out on any important restrictions that might put a damper on your plans. These requirements vary from location to location, so while we can't provide every requirement, we have posted several good resources in the index.

Now that we're diving deeper into all the things to keep in mind when choosing a space, you're probably starting to remove some of the possible locations from your lists, or shuffling them around a bit. When we said earlier that each option is a learning experience, this is exactly what we meant. A space that initially looked promising may end up being cost-prohibitive due to the operational costs, or have a lease that just doesn't make sense for your business. Financial considerations are often the number one deal breaker when it comes to choosing the right spot for your coffee shop, once all of the location needs have been met. Fear not—the right space will appear! You may have to widen your gaze, wait for exactly the right moment to pounce on the perfect property or reconsider your business plan, but this is a land of opportunity!

Step 4: Time to Go Shopping

Once you've found the ultimate space for your new coffee shop, it is appropriate to begin the process of filling it. You may have had your eye on a few things here and there while dreaming and doing research, and there's never an inappropriate time to look at your options. It's best to wait to do the actual shopping part once you've established a budget and found a solid location. Often times, it's much easier to purchase something than it is to return it, so waiting until you have firm plans in place is generally going to save you time, and potentially money.

Construction First

As mentioned earlier, you may need to do some remodeling to make the space perfect for your business. The first consideration is how you're going to accomplish that. With your floor plan in hand, determine the actual scope of your project. Are you looking at putting up a couple of shelves, or are you starting from scratch, building all of the countertops, adding electrical outlets, installing flooring, and more?

If you or someone you know well are handy, you might be tempted to take on the construction project yourself. But remember—this is a public business, subject to all sorts of codes and regulations. You'll likely need a permit for your work and have to build to the specifications of all of these regulations. The actual physical construction might be much easier than keeping up with all of the legal requirements! It may be an all-around better idea to hire a contractor for your project.

There are some advantages to hiring an independent contractor to handle your remodeling, as well as some considerations that you'll need to keep in mind. Make a list of the benefits and concerns you might encounter when going with a contractor.

PROS	CONS
Will know the legal requirements	Will be expensive
Could include remodel and design	Might have to adjust timeline
Quality is what you pay for	What if they disappear?
Will bring experience	Less hands-on
Access to larger range of resources	Might have to compromise vision

Your list of pros and cons to hiring a contractor to help you with the construction and remodeling needs in your coffee shop might look different, but these are some general considerations when thinking through the process.

Once you decide to hire a contractor, you'll need to begin the hunt to find one. First, you'll need to thoroughly research highly reputable contractors in your area. Ask family, friends, your landlord, and any trusted party for recommendations and words of caution. Read any local review sites and create a shortlist of preferred contractors. Remember—even though you may have found the perfect contractor, they may not be able to work within your timetable. Having several reliable options will help you find the perfect fit.

You'll also want to have a thorough interview with each contractor. They'll walk through estimates for the project with you, discussing the full scope of what needs to be done. Some contractors work with designers who can help you with the furniture and fixtures, in addition to construction work. This will inevitably be more expensive, but might save you a ton of stress in sourcing these items yourself. As you speak with contractors, it's important to stay true to your vision, but also to admit when you might be out of your depth when it comes to finishing and furnishing your coffee shop space.

Eventually, you will be armed with a handful of estimates and proposals. Do not immediately head for the lowest cost. Make sure the proposals include everything necessary for your project in order to avoid hidden costs. Remember, it is very rare for the estimate to be identical to the final costs of a project, so choosing the most thorough proposal may be the safest route.

As you work with your contractor, remember to be patient, and that good communication is the key to success in any project. Be honest with yourself and your contractor when you have concerns, and adhere to your budget at all times. The results will build the threshold to your very own custom coffee shop!

Go with the Flow

Once the stage is set, the next step is to add the furnishings and fixtures that will give it its full appeal. If you've done extensive construction work, you might have a lot of the fixtures already installed at this point. For those who are starting with a space that required little to no remodeling, you'll likely need to purchase everything that goes into your space, so it's time to do some shopping. Actually, it's going to be a LOT of shopping.

The shopping process begins with measurements. Lots and lots and lots of measurements. It's time to bring out the floor plan again, and you may find you need still more measurements. Consider what the interior of your coffee shop will be like when everything is in motion. The floor plan you created is the bigger picture, but now is the time to think about the smaller picture and figure out what you need to keep in mind when putting all of the moving pieces together.

Let's take your refrigerator as an example. Let's say your floor plan works best if you have three smaller refrigerators: one under the counter by the espresso machines, one next to the ice machine, and one in the back. You may be tempted to buy three identical small refrigerators, but they may not all work in their designated spaces. If the refrigerator door is too wide or opens too far, it might bang into another shelving area, or render another piece of equipment unusable, or hold up workers walking by. If the nearest electrical outlet is three feet away, a refrigerator that has a two-foot cord will not work. Taking these seemingly insignificant details into consideration now will save you from a lot of heartache and scrambling for a solution at the last minute.

Much like the staff you eventually hire, all the pieces inside your coffee shop have to work together in harmony. Putting a sofa by the door won't work if the door will constantly slam into the legs of someone sitting there. These are the types of measurements you need to consider when planning your shopping list.

Define Your Style

When you're making your shopping list, it might be easy to write "a sofa" on your list. After the last step, hopefully, that line item has been updated to "a sofa, maximum 6-feet long." In this step, you'll refer back to the business plan to define that even further.

If you are opening a coffee shop in which you expect guests to come in and spend some time, the style of your shop should be cohesive and consistent. It should be inviting, and make people feel comfortable. Customers should want to spend time there.

Your style is your own. Perhaps you want a bohemian feel. Maybe streamlined and stainless steel is your preference. You might be going for that leather-and-mahogany library feel. Whatever your style is, here are some things to keep in mind when adding furniture to your shopping list:

- Customers expect clean furniture. A white velvet sofa may be beautiful, but it will be stained almost instantly. Make sure surfaces can be easily cleaned, stain treated, and meet fire code.

- Customers don't want wobbly furniture. You might find some discount cafe tables online, but make sure they assemble perfectly and provide a level, solid surface.
- Customers will spill. Customers will neglect to use coasters. When considering surfaces on tables, chairs, and the floor, think of what that surface can tolerate. If you put rugs on the floor, how will they get cleaned when a large decaf gets dumped on them? If you purchase wooden tables, are they treated to tolerate moisture, heat, and cold?
- If you have free-standing lamps, how heavy are they? Can they be knocked over easily? Would they cause a serious injury if they fell on a foot, or worse—a child?
- Speaking of children, if you plan to make your establishment child-friendly, can the furniture handle a full load of toys, crayons, markers, and more? If your tables are ruined by a single permanent marker accident, they may not be the best investment for a coffee shop that encourages children to visit.

These are just some things to keep in mind first and foremost. As you build your shopping list for the interior of your coffee shop, you may want to make a line item list that takes all of these pieces into consideration. Be as specific as you need to be!

For example, your shopping list may look like this:

ITEM (QTY)	SIZE	COLOR	NOTES
Sofa/loveseat (2)	6-8 feet long	Maroon, dark brown	Leather sofa, modern style
Coffee Table (2)	4-5 feet long	Dark woodgrain, black	To match sofa, modern style
Cafe Tables (8)	3-foot diameter	Dark woodgrain, black	No more than 36" high, room to seat two guests, round only.
Cafe Seats (16)	Standard, light-weight	Silver/metal	Slatted back, modern look
Bookcase (2)	8 feet tall, 4 feet wide, no deeper than 16 inches	Dark woodgrain, black	Modern look, adjustable shelves, not top heavy—must be solid or wall anchor

In essence, you want your shopping list to include every term you would consider entering in an online search for that object. Add every item that will help your vision come to life, as well as any considerations for ensuring that the item is safe and enjoyable for your environment.

The Big Supplies

Shopping for your new coffee shop extends beyond furniture and appliances, of course. You won't be able to serve customers if you don't have all the supplies you need. This includes everything from cups, lids, and stir sticks, to toilet paper, soap, and floor mats.

You'll need to think through the entire process each time you intend to buy. Not only will you need napkins, you'll need dispensers to hold them. If you're serving food in-house, you'll need not just dishes, but bins to collect dirty dishes, chemicals to wash the dishes, a place to wash dishes, a place to store the dishes, and so on. You may wish to use exclusively disposable service products, including plastic utensils and paper plates, but bear in mind, it will become expensive very quickly. It's also not environmentally friendly, which may alienate some of your customer base.

The kitchen is a very important location for supplies. You'll need chemicals to disinfect all the surfaces, sanitize the dishes, and wash the floors, for example. You'll need handwashing stations, and possibly plastic gloves for food handling. You'll need health department signage hung conspicuously for staff, which is regulated by the state health department. You'll need bar towels to clean up messes, which will also need laundering.

Depending on your location, there may be services that can deliver these items to you on a regular basis. While you may feel confident you can run to the store any time you need more bathroom supplies or napkins, be realistic about your schedule. If you spend all day at the coffee shop, when are you going to feel like getting supplies? When are the stores in your area open? Buying in bulk is always more cost-efficient, so do you have a bulk shop close to you? What membership requirements do they have? Sure, you could probably request a delivery from Amazon or InstaCart in a pinch, but the delivery and service fees aren't necessarily dollars you'll be able to spend at first.

Check the internet for some of the popular companies that provide service in your area, and really take a look at the scope of their services. Some can help with creating logo napkins and to-go cups. Some can wash and replace linens, uniforms, doormats, and stock the bathroom all in one visit. While there will, of course, be fees associated with these services, it's a great idea to do the research and price out what that would cost versus trying to do it all on your own. Sure, you can run to Costco three times a week now, but what happens when you run out of medium cups during a holiday season rush? Peace of mind is difficult to price, so be conscious of your budget and adjust accordingly.

Appliances Big and Small

When considering appliances, there are loads of little details that you may not have considered yet. Sure, you've got a list of what you need, what size, and details like color and plug length, but lots of appliances work a lot of different ways, and all of those functions impact price.

Do you know how much a cafe-style espresso machine costs? The answer is that it can vary, greatly. Depending on how many shots you want to be able to pour at once, you could be looking at hundreds or thousands of dollars. That can mean only one thing—back to the internet for research!

You'll find there are loads of suppliers out there. In fact, many food services offer equipment for sale as well. You can find used equipment, equipment to rent, or choose brand new equipment. Many experienced restaurant owners will caution against used equipment, as it is hard to judge exactly how reliable a used coffee maker may be, for example. It is possible to find great deals, though, so researching these options isn't out of the question. Just be sure to be extra cautious when reviewing any type of appliance. The best value will be a mix of reliability, functionality, safety, and price.

As you shop, also keep in mind that you will need to keep continuous maintenance on every appliance you purchase. Not only does the appliance's dependability rely on it, but health codes may require regular maintenance. Commercial-style refrigerators, for example, can require full cleaning and maintenance that can be very expensive. Before you go all-out on a variety of appliances, consider what you truly need for your first year of business and go from there. Your budget—and your stress level—will thank you.

An Important Reminder and a Second Pep Talk:

Preparing for the opening of your very own coffee shop probably hasn't been a walk in the park so far. You've had to come up with a business plan. You've gone through the rigorous process of financing your operation. It's likely taken you much longer than you anticipated to find just the right location, and you've poured lots of time and money into purchasing all of the right furniture and fixtures for your coffee shop. You may feel a little overwhelmed or discouraged many times throughout the process, but that is entirely normal. There will be good days amongst the bad, and your dreams will eventually come true. One of the wisest statements shared amongst business owners is that, as long as you do something to make progress every single day, even if it doesn't get the results you anticipated, you're still headed in the right direction. Something that may seem small, like hanging a picture on the walls or deciding what you want the countertops to look like, may feel insignificant, but they are still steps toward your Grand Opening.

Step 5: Bringing in the Product

At this point, you've got your location, you've got your seating and appliances, and it's time to make the really, really big decision: What do you serve?

Who You Serve Is What You Serve

One very important rule of thumb in the restaurant business is that what you serve has to match the people who buy it. It's time to revisit the business plan in earnest, especially the section about "Who Is Your Clientele?" Let's walk through a few examples of how who you serve impacts what you serve.

Example A: Your city has a Coffee Festival. You want to be included in this festival. As a result, you'll need to serve the most unique, delicious coffee in the area to gain recognition. You'll want to look at exotic coffees, or perhaps roast your own beans in-house (which means additional equipment, of course!). You're not going to settle for "just whatever;" instead, you're going to search the ends of the Earth to source the most unique coffee. As a result, you'll have a higher price tag than any old neighborhood coffee shop, but you'll have a clientele that is willing to pay for a coffee experience, rather than just a caffeinated drink.

Example B: As a coffee shop that caters to the community, you've decided that you really want to be eco-friendly, which has gained the attention of certain groups in the community. They want to use your coffee shop as a meeting spot, and after spending time with them, you have learned that they appreciate organic and vegan products. In this case, you're going to need to serve plenty of organic coffee options. While you may not serve strictly organic beverages and food, you will want to make sure that you have many choices for these customers.

Example C: You want to build a family-friendly coffee shop, where moms and dads can meet up, and children can interact and have fun. In this case, having exclusive coffee beans isn't nearly as important as having drinks that can be made quickly, thoroughly customized, and are generally inexpensive to create. You'll want a menu that's chock-full of fun drinks for kids, too, perhaps without the espresso. You may look at having more blended drinks, which means an ice maker and lots of milk and not-so-exotic syrups and flavors.

As you can see, the quality and quantity of coffee you purchase depends heavily on who will be doing the drinking. In Example A, you may have smaller quantities of very high-quality coffee. In Example B, you will likely have a substantial amount of tasty organic coffee, but the quality is not nearly as significant as the fact that it is organic. In Example C, the quality of the coffee doesn't matter nearly as much as having plenty of it, backing the sweet zip of caffeine with drink recipes that are imaginative and cater to a wide audience.

A Snack to Suit the Crowd

Any food you may choose to serve will then have to match the coffee. If you're pursuing a gourmet experience, such as in Example A, it would not make sense to have super-basic food. Your customers are going to want a full gourmet experience, so consider pairing this type of coffee with treats that also have that gourmet flair. You may wish to include charcuterie or cheese plates, which can be tasty treat any time of day and coordinated for any meal. You may wish to serve pastries that have a bit of an international flair. Macarons, for example, are a French delight that can be flavored with very high-class ingredients. For those who have an organic-centric menu, such as in Example B, you'll want to continue this commitment and include food options that are organic and vegan. You're going to need organic milk and non-dairy milk options, too. If the patrons of your coffee shop are going to include children, like Example C, you'll want snacks that are easy to hold and easy to clean up. Favorites include cookies, fruit and veggies, or simple sandwiches.

The important thing to remember when creating your menu is that you cannot possibly have everything that every customer wants. Repeat this to yourself many, many times:

> *I cannot run a business that provides everything everyone wants every time.*

It's strictly impossible. Sure, it's great to offer gluten-free, dairy-free, nut-free, and vegan options. But your budget will suffer if you try to make sure you have every version of every dish. If you have carrot, blueberry, and oat muffins, you may wish to carry blueberry muffins in a gluten-free option as well. At some point, someone will be disappointed that you do not have a gluten-free carrot muffin. While the customer's frustration is understandable, you simply cannot carry absolutely everything all at once. You can't store it. You can't order it week after week in hopes that someone will want it. Above all, you can't afford to waste it.

When you're brainstorming recipes, try to use ingredients several times. For example, if you plan on offering a cafe mocha, you'll need chocolate syrup. That same chocolate syrup can be used in countless signature drinks, as topping on blended or iced drinks, as an ingredient in chocolate milk or hot cocoa, and so on. Always use your imagination when coming up with your menu, but try to work with as few unique ingredients as possible. This will save you in many ways: you won't have to store as many products. You won't have to buy as many products. And most of all, you won't have to waste as many products.

So, let's say you really want to create a frozen chocolate and banana drink. Whether you use real bananas or banana-flavored syrup, you'll have to buy that in addition to the chocolate, coffee, and milk. Now let's say you sell one of those drinks each day. Now check the expiration date on the syrup, or glumly watch the bananas languish and turn brown. If you incorporate that banana taste in several other drinks, it won't be wasted, and the cost will make sense for your business model!

Considering the Overall Menu

When first starting your coffee shop, it's really best to keep it simple. Doing a few things very well is going to attract far more customers than doing a lot of things frantically. Every recipe you concoct is going to require not only ingredients, but also time to make it, time to serve it, and time to train staff how to make it. And remember this very important idea: You can ALWAYS add more. As time goes by and your business flourishes, you'll get an even better idea for what customers love. Maybe some interesting frequent drink orders will make it onto the menu as regular offerings. Don't exhaust your creativity before you even open your doors. Start simple with some guaranteed crowd pleasers, and perhaps a handful of signature drinks. That creativity will be your ultimate tool in helping business continue to flourish as the customer base grows!

Make your menu flexible, as well. Each customer is going to have different tastes, dietary requirements, and possible allergies. Consider possible add-ons, like an extra flavor shot, specialty milk, adding cheese to a sandwich, and more. What options and upgrades will you provide? What will you charge for these upgrades? Don't go overboard with the options, but make it flexible, so that the customer who can't have dairy can order almond milk, or so the customer who doesn't like banana but loves caramel can have that instead. This is not in contradiction to the earlier advice regarding having too many options, but adjacent to it. You are not adding options to your menu, you are simply replacing one thing with another thing you have in stock already.

Sourcing Coffee

Where will you find your coffee? It may seem that the options are endless. A Google search will lead you down a rabbit hole of options, but it is a very good way to get a feel of some of the available choices. At the same time, you may have a few good resources closer to your coffee shop.

Some coffee shops roast their own beans. This means you'll have to find a source of raw coffee beans and the equipment for roasting, as well as the knowledge and expertise in the roasting process, which is a little more in-depth than watching a YouTube video a few times. Unless you already have this experience, you may want to work your business up to this process.

Perhaps you have a local coffee roaster in your city or state. If you enjoy their product and it fits with your business model, you may wish to reach out to them regarding their wholesale capabilities. Please note that while many roasters will be thrilled by the opportunity, some smaller businesses may simply lack the capacity to produce regular large orders. As you work with this roaster, you'll agree upon a price, transport of the beans from their business to yours, and any cross-promotion or marketing you'll do for each other. You've likely seen signs that state "Proudly Serving (Brand)" at various coffee shops, which is an indication that the proprietor is doing the exact same thing.

Lastly, there are wholesale opportunities, even for gourmet coffee! Many food services offer upscale coffee, but there are several companies dedicated specifically to supplying coffee shops and venues that specialize in coffee. Take a look at some of these options when making your sourcing decisions, because you will likely find a few tasty beans which you might not have even thought about! Additionally, these services have serious expertise, and while you'll be paying a higher amount to have their roasted beans delivered to you, this can be extremely cost-effective in the long run, especially when first starting out.

Creating Vs. Assembling Vs. Purchasing

Once you've finalized the menu, it's time to figure out how the treats you've decided upon are going to make it from your imagination to the customer's hands. The three most popular models for adding food to your menu are Creating, Assembling, and Purchasing. Some coffee shops use one model exclusively, while others use a little bit of each method. Here are a few of the things to consider about each option:

- Creating means baking from scratch. If you choose this method, you'll need:
- Recipes
- All of the ingredients
- Storage for the ingredients
- Equipment for stirring, mixing, baking, etc.
- Room for laying out ingredients, mixing, and putting together baking sheets
- A staff member to have baking completed by opening. Typically, a baker will work overnight to ensure the products are as fresh as possible by the time your doors open for the day.

Naturally, all of these elements have practical and financial considerations. Buying and storing ingredients such as flour, sugar, and butter, is very inexpensive and simple, and these individual ingredients typically have a long shelf life. This translates into less waste. At the same time, you'll have to pay a staff member to come in for a few hours every night to make the goodies. You'll have to make sure they're trained and properly equipped.

Assembling means you'll have pieces and parts of your menu items on hand, which can be put together or heated upon request. You'll need:

- Each piece of the item for assembly. For example, if you want to have Danish on the menu, you could purchase frozen pastry shells and filling.
- Room to assemble
- The equipment to combine ingredients or bake, which could include ovens, pans, sandwich presses, or soup urns

These are going to be more expensive and require more slightly more intense storage than dry ingredients, with a shorter shelf life, but you'll have the ability to make each product to order, which will help keep waste down. You'll also be able to quickly train staff to assemble each treat according to your specifications, so there will be no need for an additional staff member.

Lastly, there's always the option to purchase your treats. Some coffee shops prefer working with local bakeries or eateries to bring in their products daily. This could range from having this other business make all of the food for your coffee shop, or perhaps just elements, for example, loaves of bread. Contracting with local companies is a great way to establish yourself in the community. By carrying a brand name that is already known and loved, the customers of that brand will be intrigued by your new enterprise. You and the other business owner can cross-promote and host events together, which will be a very fun and simple way to gain business in your community.

Another option for purchasing treats is to check out the offerings of wholesale food retailers. Perhaps your supply service also offers gourmet treats, which can be stored, refrigerated or frozen (depending on type and ingredients), and served with little to no preparation. This is going to be the most expensive option at the outset because you're purchasing a fully prepared product. These items will likely have a very short shelf life since they're ready to eat, but you most likely won't need any supplies other than perhaps a microwave oven to briefly thaw or reheat the item.

When purchasing your food, you'll either sell out very quickly, or experience a significant amount of waste. You'll also need more space for refrigeration, which as you may recall from the earlier section, requires a great deal of maintenance and attention to keep it up to health code. Some restaurant owners report that keeping a walk-in cooler fully compliant can cost several thousand dollars each inspection period. When factoring in the high cost of ready to eat food, plus the cost of adequate refrigeration, you'll likely have very little room for profit, or be forced to charge a significant amount more than customers are willing to spend.

Regardless of which option you choose, you will need to find a supplier for your food or ingredients. Some areas are lucky enough to have a local restaurant wholesaler, which will allow you to peruse the stock and get a feel for the taste and quality of their products before committing to a regular order. If not, have no fear—there are a variety of national companies that supply restaurants nearly everywhere.

As with every other purchase you've made, you'll need to do a lot of research and a little shopping around for the best options and deals. Value is, again, not just choosing the least expensive option. The best option may not be the most expensive. Evaluate everything not only by price, but by how easy or difficult it is to store it, how labor intensive it is to produce it, and of course, how good it tastes.

One very important hint that chefs around the world swear by is to Taste Everything. Don't sell
something unless you can personally vouch for its taste and quality. Furthermore, don't just taste it yourself. Taste is hugely subjective, so invite friends and family to help you with taste tests. You may repeat these tests more than once, so gather a group of people with very different taste buds and preferences!

Tasting things helps you decide exactly how to make them in a manner that most customers will enjoy. You will need to refine your recipes down to the quantity of each ingredient for each item made, so make sure that you have the perfect amount of flavor syrup, the perfect water-to-bean ratio, the right fineness when grinding beans, the most delicious filtered water, and the right number of blueberries in your scones. Quantity translates into inventory, so consider the cost of each ingredient when adding it to your recipes.

You may be very tempted to choose the cheapest option on the market, and sometimes, that might be perfectly fine. Often, things like sugar packets or non-dairy creamer are roughly the same no matter which brand or supplier you choose.

There are many instances, however, in which quality is required. If your baked goods taste dry because you bought them on the "day old" rack, no one will buy them, and your reputation will suffer. If your coffee tastes burnt, you'll sell less of it. If your blended drinks aren't sweet enough, or no one can actually taste the banana in your chocolate-banana drink, it's not good enough to sell. Don't cut corners—create a menu that is lively, and that offers quality that matches both the experience and the price. This is yet another way you can avoid waste.

On the Topic of Waste

Waste is a very common and unavoidable topic when serving food or beverages of any kind. There are many ways in which waste can occur, and it may not be something you can prevent. Here are some of the most common forms of waste:

Preventable waste:
- Serving the customer the wrong product
- Having more inventory than you can sell
- Improper storage
- Improper handling

Unpreventable waste:
- Customer tries the product but doesn't like it
- Power outage
- Accidentally spilling, dropping, overheating, or otherwise making the product unsaleable
- Spoiling too soon or arriving damaged

As you can see, waste can happen even under the best intentions. If you are familiar with any type of produce, you'll know that there is always the chance that the apples or grapes will go bad long before you expect them to. Food simply isn't designed to be limitless, so you will find yourself throwing out food despite storing and handling everything properly.

At the same time, there are some very definite steps you can take to ensure you aren't swimming in waste. Try to be scrupulous when ordering inventory, for example. The general rule about inventory is that you won't have it perfected until your third year of business. When starting out, you are literally going to be guessing about quantities and amounts of everything. You'll learn a little more each month, and certain patterns will slowly start to reveal themselves. In the food industry, almost every single business owner will confess that they've had to run to the local grocery store at some time in their career due to running out of an essential item.

Remember, it is far more cost effective to run out of a product, apologize, and offer the customer a similar item, than it is to throw away large quantities of stock because it didn't sell.

When creating your recipes, be specific about amounts, and make sure you have the equipment to help your future staff measure correctly. If your recipe says "6 ounces of milk," make sure they know how much 6 ounces really is, either with measuring cups, or marked cups used specifically for measuring. Don't switch it up, either: if your recipe calls for 2 ounces of syrup, don't tell workers, "that's, like, two or three pumps." Consistency reduces waste. If every drink and food item is made the exact same way every single time, barring accidents, the customer will receive identical product every single time, and you'll be able to accurately measure how much of each product you're using daily.

Additionally, it's important to pay attention to the rules you'll learn when earning your ServSafe certification. This required certification for those serving and handling food items will help you gauge the best ways to store, assemble, create, and serve any food and beverage your coffee shop sells. Health code adherence will also teach you some important things, such as how quickly the steamed milk should be cooled, which products can be left out of the refrigerator for how long, and which products have the potential to make many people very sick.

At this point, you'll have your stack of drink and food recipes in one hand, and your budget in the other. While we have provided some handy references in the index, this list is not exhaustive. Depending on your location and network, you may have many more resources available to you. Creativity is a necessity when it comes to owning a business, as you have likely learned by now. Find multiple solutions for each supply requirement, and soon you'll have put together all of the pieces that make up your supply chain.

Step 6: The Wild World of Marketing

Sure, there are marketing geniuses out there, but many smaller businesses, especially those who cater to a smaller community rather than the whole wide world, are perfectly capable of handling marketing in-house. Marketing has a reputation for being a bit of a wild world, perhaps due to the ever-changing landscape of what's in, what's out, what's trending, what's now considered passe, etc. Do not allow yourself to become paralyzed by fear at the word "marketing."

If you have already started spreading the word in the community, you've already started marketing. If you have a sign outside your location that says "Coming soon..." you've already started marketing. See? That wasn't so hard! The next few steps will take a little strategy and attention, but don't worry—the internet is absolutely flooded with helpful guides to marketing. Here are our very simple rules for researching marketing on the internet:

- DO: Research one topic at a time.
- DO: Take notes or print off any step-by-step guides.
- DON'T: Go down the rabbit hole. Everything you read will link to twenty other topics. Stay on task.
- DON'T: Take everything as a law. Red may be THE color for this season, but in two weeks, blue might suddenly be the attention color. These are not rules, they are suggestions.

That being said, here are some helpful hints for various marketing avenues that you may wish to pursue in order to give your new coffee shop the attention it needs. It is highly recommended that you start the marketing process well before you open your doors. Build excitement and anticipation for your new business!

Sign Here

Signage is very important. It tells people where your shop is located. It sets the very first impression of your shop. Your logo and sign are your very first communication with your future customers, so make it count. Choose fonts and colors that truly represent your coffee shop, and that match your vision and plan. For example, if you're looking to establish a gourmet experience, you won't want signage in Comic Sans. Instead, you'll want images and fonts that convey a truly elegant location.

The size of your signage and logo are also important. Simple names and logos can be printed in a variety of sizes, even quite small. Think of some of the most iconic logos of our time. Even if you were to see the McDonald's Golden Arches printed the size of this text, you would still associate it with the fast-food restaurant. A more complicated logo, however, will lose focus as it becomes smaller, with intricate details getting kicked out as the pixel count decreases. Make sure your sign is readable, and that your logo doesn't turn into a smudge when viewed from afar, or in a smaller format.

You may wish to hire a designer to help you nail down the details of your logo, especially if you're feeling less than artistic. There are also many websites that can help you with this process. Granted, you'll need to tap into the budget once again, but many online logo services are reasonably priced, and will help you build a lasting logo that will help your business become readily recognizable for years to come.

Www. You're Going to Build a Website. Com

In this day and age, creating a website is an inevitable requirement for nearly every business. People will hear your business name, and they'll head to their smartphone to look up important information like hours of operation, days that you're open, and an idea of what you serve. This is reasonable information to request, and it makes sense to give the people what they need. After all, you want to give them absolutely every reason to show up for fresh scones at 6 am on Monday morning!

There are tons of ways to create websites, but perhaps one of the most popular and easy-for-nearly-everybody site builders is WordPress. WordPress is inexpensive, it's popular, it includes a lot of freebies to help you get started, and it involves really simple aspects like drag-and-drop images and videos.

Whatever platform you choose for your website, you can decide to be as elaborate as you want; however, there are certain factors which you need to have displayed in a way that customers can very clearly find them, even when they are under-caffeinated and blearily making their way to your parking lot. These include:

- Your logo
- What kind of business you are
- Your address
- Your hours of operation
- A few pictures
- A page which displays a menu
- (example: http://www.riverroadcoffeehouse.com/)

When adding photos and content to your website, there are a few things to keep in mind. First, you want all content to be "evergreen." That means that for the most part, you will rarely have to change this content, if ever. Things like your photo and biography are evergreen. Your address and any Google map link you choose to add to it won't change. When uploading menu information, make sure you include top sellers and products you plan to offer continuously. You are more than welcome to update your website with the "Special of the Week" or the "Pastry of the Day," but remember, that means you will have to update that information every time it changes, or you'll gain a reputation for having an out-of-date website.

Using your own images is always the safest option, and in this day of smartphones with built-in cameras, it is extremely easy. While you may yearn for those beautiful, fine-tuned photos you see on the websites of more established websites, you'll have to make sure you have it in your budget to hire a professional photographer. You may wish to incorporate some images taken by other professionals into your website but beware: most photographers or businesses have copyrighted their photos, which means you absolutely cannot use them to promote your business without permission. Stock photos are an option, and frequently free or very inexpensive. Always give credit where credit is due, so if you incorporate another party's image, make sure you give them photo credit.

Having an out-of-date website can be a problem for a few reasons. First, customers won't like it. They'll completely call you out if the Pastry of the Day has been a pistachio muffin for six months. Secondly, it reflects poorly on you as a business owner. Visitors to your website will wonder what's wrong with business that you don't have time to change a single line of text (which makes it worth mentioning—many sites, including WordPress—can be accessed via your mobile). They may question the reliability of other information on your website, including hours of operation, and decide not to stop by. Lastly, these types of inaccuracies can reflect poorly on your Google ratings. If people go to your website and get incorrect information, they'll stop going to your website. If they stop going to your website, it will become buried under other local options, so when folks in your area search for "coffee shop near me," your shop will not be at the top of the list. You definitely want to be at the top of the list!

"Stellar content!" is one of the most popular marketing battle cries, and for good reason. Your website is absolutely worthless if the content isn't intelligent, entertaining, and full of accurate information. There are several ways you can communicate content to folks through your website, and how deep you want to go depends on your overall goals for your business. Note: You do not have to give these pages the specific names—these are categories, more than titles! Be yourself!

1. An "About" page. For most businesses, having an About page is a great idea. Not only does this allow people to read more and linger on your page, which drives up those Google ratings, but it gives people an idea of who you are, and what your business is about. It humanizes you and personalizes the experience for all your customers. You don't have to go into a great deal—typically, 300-500 words is enough.

2. An "Experience" page. This page will tell the audience what to expect when they walk into your coffee shop. "When you walk into my coffee shop, your senses will be enrobed in the aroma of fresh-brewed coffee from around the world." This is where you can paint a picture of your vision to share with people and draw them in. Make them think they can't possibly pass up on your coffee! Tell them whose beans you sell, or your roasting process. Get them as excited as you are about your coffee shop.

3. An "Events" page. This is only important if you are going to actually host events or happenings at your coffee shop, but it can be useful for attracting attention to anything fun that might draw a larger crowd. If you're having a paint night, for example, let people know. If the local Kiwanis will be there every Thursday night, put it on the calendar. The benefit of this is that people will be able to pick a great time to experience your coffee shop and know when might not be the best time. If the Kiwanis are meeting, a harried mother may not want to drag the entire soccer team to your shop after practice, for example.

4. A Menu. You can either post your menu as an image or link to a PDF folks can download. As mentioned earlier, you might want

to make this relatively non-specific, especially at first, when you're finding what works best for your business. Adding simple things like "House Blend - a delicious 100% Kenyan blend, roasted at nearby place" will suffice, as well as the price per size. If you're not fully sure what specific pastries you'll have on hand, "A rotating selection of fine treats and snacks—ask your barista for more information!" will be perfect. If you don't serve food at all, this is also a great time to mention it, so that someone who has a hankering for a snack doesn't let loose their hanger (that's their anger from hunger) on you!

5. A Blog. Now we're getting into some of the more elaborate functions, but there are a couple of really good reasons you might want to feature a blog on your website, especially before opening.

    a. First, that content will set the scene for prospective customers. Yes, you've painted a pretty picture in the "Experience" page, but the blog is a journey. You can post about how exciting it was, trying to source the perfect beans. You can post pictures of the entire process of setting up the space. You are basically telling the story of your coffee shop here. You are explaining to your audience the who, when, where, what, and how of the entire vision and plan that you started with in the very first step. This draws them in and makes them more emotionally and personally invested in your coffee shop.

    b. Next, a blog improves Google ratings. The more time someone spends on your website, the higher the Google rating!

    c. Having this information made public will also gain attention. As chatter spreads about your upcoming Grand Opening, you might have the media reach out to you, including local websites, newspapers, groups, etc. By having accurate information prominently displayed on your website, you have already taken the first step in revealing yourself to the community, and this information might be featured in any media reports about your location.

d. Social media crossover. We're about to talk more about social media, but one very nice feature of blog posts is that you can link to them from any other social media, so, instead of having to write several different posts each time you update social media, you can simply write, "Check out our latest blog post here!" with a link. Easy as can be!

e. Make sure your social media links are also posted on your website, too. Make it as easy as possible for people to find every shred of information they may wish to discover about your shop!

Follow Us On…

Nearly everyone and their grandmother can be found on some level of social media these days. Facebook, Instagram, and Twitter seem to be the "big three" of this decade, but given the fickle nature of social media, that could change in an instant. For now, let's focus on using social media in a constructive way… though maybe not an "out of the box creative" way.

Let's start with Facebook. Having a business page on Facebook takes a little bit of patience to set up, but once you do, you'll be able to start networking, advertising, and drawing in the community right away! The beauty of Facebook is that you can post all sorts of things to gain the attention of your community—photos, text, videos, events, and more. People can comment and interact with your posts, which will bump them up in the mysterious Facebook algorithm so that more and more people see your posts. People will also be able to share your posts with each other, drawing more and more followers to your page.

To start your brand new Facebook page, visit www.facebook.com/business. From there, you'll be asked all kinds of questions about your business. Answer these questions honestly, as the information you provide will be published in the profile of your page. This is important because people trying to learn more about your business will land there. Make it easy for them!

Next, you'll want to upload some pictures. Your logo makes a great user pic. A picture of your storefront or sign makes an excellent cover photo. Since you're establishing a coffee shop, add a bunch of pictures that are rich in coffee content.

Now what about content? Obviously, you will want to mention as many times as possible when you plan to open. You will want to make it abundantly clear where you are located, and what you serve. Just like the landing page of your website, you don't want people to have to search for clues.

At the same time, you'll want to be engaging. Sticking within the theme and vision of your coffee shop, consider posting memes about coffee, links to news articles about coffee, videos that explain some of the ins and outs of coffee that your regular drinker might not know. Inform. Educate. Entertain. The goal is to have people share your posts with other people, which will gain more exposure for you and your coffee shop!

What about Instagram? Instagram is all about the pictures. Chances are high that you won't update this account as frequently as your Facebook. There is no perfect frequency of updates that will magically create the perfect number of customers. A lot of it depends on your community, your audience, and how you network. However, posting quality content to Instagram is just as important. You don't have to be a professional photographer to get attention on Instagram; besides, the most important part is gathering followers.

Twitter can be harder to master for new initiates. With its shorter word count and compressed messages, as well as a constantly moving tide of trending topics, it's hard to stay on top of what's important on Twitter. Don't despair, though: one easy trick on Twitter is linking the photos you use on Instagram or the posts you make on Facebook to your Twitter account. This will keep your feed constantly refreshed without having to count letters and characters. You can also link to any specials or blog posts that you include on your website.

So how do you get followers? One tried-and-true method is to start with the people you already know. Send requests to all of your friends and family. Even if they don't live in the same community, they can pass on the link to your accounts to their friends and family. This is the very basic formation of a network.

Next, link up with local or community Facebook groups. Does your town have a restaurant owners' group? How about local foodie groups? Any community bulletin board groups? Some neighborhoods have their own Facebook groups, and many would love to hear about a new coffee shop in their area. Linking up with groups will expand your visibility past friends and into the community.

What about Facebook ads? Boosting a post on Facebook is relatively inexpensive, and you have the option of setting demographic specifications when doing so. This is a true case of "you get what you pay for," because Facebook will explain exactly how many days and how many people will be able to see your ad, based on the ad level you purchase. There's no guarantee that all of those people will care, or that any of those people will appear at your coffee shop, looking to try your delicious beverages. It's not a bad idea to boost your posts once in a while, as long as you can afford the audience range you really want. At minimum, Facebook users will see your logo in their feed, which may eventually lead them to check out your shop.

Important Things to Avoid on Social Media

Since so many people are on social media in some capacity, you will likely encounter some troublesome individuals and some uncomfortable situations. As a business owner, it is most beneficial for the overall success of your business that your social media accounts are a neutral place. That means you must present the cleanest, most un-opinionated material possible. That means:

- No politics
- No controversial current events (unless unavoidable—such as a road closure that will impact your business)
- No arguing or engaging with argumentative customers. When people say rude, obnoxious, or obviously inflammatory comments on your page, we strongly recommend taking those conversations out of the public eye. In fact, if you can convince that individual to call you directly, even better. It's important to address their concerns (unless absolutely off-the-wall), but doing so in the public eye, where screenshots can spread like wildfire, is an incredibly bad idea.
- No inappropriate language or images
- No bad-mouthing the competition
- Stay positive at all times

Once you become a community mainstay, you might begin to feel a little too comfortable with your internet family. Avoid doing anything that might be construed as controversial, and you should have no problems navigating a successful social media presence.

The Method of Our Forefathers

One of the most timeless methods of marketing is just getting out there, physically. Having an actual physical presence is more than just putting up a few "Coming Soon" signs or hanging your official store sign. You need to advertise more than out of the corner of someone's eye as they drive by.

Consider printing up flyers with your logo, your address, and Grand Opening information. Depending on your local ordinances, there are many ways you can distribute these amongst your community to let them know that your business is coming soon. Some establishments may allow you to hang small posters announcing your opening. Never assume that businesses will allow your flyers or posters—always ask before hanging.

As we mentioned in the section regarding funding options, getting out into the neighborhood via events and gatherings is a great idea. You also may wish to join the local Chamber of Commerce, or business association, or one of many possible groups in which local business owners network and discuss current events. Becoming acquaintances with other local business owners prior to opening will help you gain a welcome entry into the community, and you may use these connections to your favor in the future.

All the Right Stuff

Then there's the matter of merchandising. Proudly displaying your logo in your community is a great idea, but where's the sweet spot of "stuff"?

When it comes to merchandising, one of the most popular items businesses sell are logo t-shirts. These are pretty simple to acquire, as there are many sites across the internet that will allow you to upload your logo, and for a fee, print your logo on a variety of merchandise. This fee can vary greatly, depending on the type and quantity of merchandise. The rules may be different for different shops. Some base your order on total number of items ordered (say, 14 t-shirts and 14 mugs), while others have bulk pricing per type of item.

At first, you may wish to purchase very little merchandise. While it's a great moneymaker, chances are low that people will buy a t-shirt from an unestablished business. At the same time, if you're purchasing a bunch of logo shirts for your staff, for example, purchasing a few extra will likely bring the price-per-shirt down. The same is true if you're making logo coffee mugs for your shop. Adding a few to the count might offer you a better price on your overall order, which you can recoup by selling them to customers in your shop.

Generally speaking, small items are a safe bet. Things like stickers or decals, even pins or buttons are inexpensive when bought in bulk and can be handed out or sold to customers. These items take up very little room, as well, so you won't sacrifice much storage or display space, either. Make sure that whatever merchandise you invest in can be neatly displayed, can be stored in a clean, safe place, and carries a level of interest to your customers. Sure, it might be fun to have skateboards with your logo printed on them, but do you or your customers actually need a skateboard? (If skating is your theme, then of course, that might be a "yes"!)

The goal of marketing is to get your name into the public, excite and draw in customers, and establish a positive reputation in your community. These suggestions are hardly exhaustive; if anything, they should inspire you to think of other options that will help you connect your community with the business you will soon be opening.

As the years go by, your marketing plan may change and develop. Trends may be very different two years from now, so one important factor in a successful marketing plan is flexibility. At some point, you may wish to consult with a professional, depending on how quickly your business grows. On the other hand, your business might be designed to stay small and local. Every community is different, and there may be some ways to announce your business that are unique to your area. In order to build a brand in your area, you will have to become a part of the neighborhood. A successful marketing program will make your brand, your logo, and your coffee shop familiar to as much of your town or city as possible. As word spreads, the number of customers who visit your shop will increase. They, in turn, will mention the positive experience they have had at your coffee shop with their friends, family, coworkers, and neighbors. Before long, you'll be the talk of town, as everyone stops by to check out the "new kid on the block." These first few months will be intense, and very important for making first impressions amongst your customer base. You will want to put on your best face, so to speak, in every element of your business.

Step 7: The Hiring and Staffing Process

An Important Note about Labor Laws

Before we get started with this chapter, we'd like to mention that there are a lot of legal considerations that go into the staffing process. There are federal employment regulations and state employment regulations. These laws and regulations can cover everything from how often employees must go on break, to how many hours they can work per week. There are things like taxes, workers' compensation, unemployment payments, and who is legally permitted to work for you, all of which must be considered during the hiring process. There will be forms to fill out, all of which bear mysterious, non-specific numeral names, like I9, W2, 1099, and more.

The hiring and staffing process is one in which you can get into a lot of trouble by disobeying the laws. Something as simple as failing to display current labor laws in a prominent area accessed by all staff can earn you serious fines that can jeopardize your coffee shop's ability to stay open. We strongly recommend not taking any chances with fumbling any of these legalities. There are resources that are well-versed in the law, including Human Resources consultants or lawyers, to ensure that any practices you are following throughout this process are 100% legal. At the very minimum, you will need to:

- Obtain an Employee Identification Number (EIN) from the IRS
- Register with your State Department of Labor
- Sign up for Workers' Compensation Insurance
- Set up a payroll system that will withhold taxes
- Make yourself familiar with all the laws that impact your business and your employees, including Title VII of the Civil Rights Act of 1964, The Age Discrimination in Employment Act of 1967, The Americans with Disabilities Act of 1990, and The Family Medical Leave Act of 1993

Knowing the legalities of employment won't make the process any easier, but you will be able to rest, knowing that you are working within the requirements of the law.

When it comes to hiring new personnel, you might feel a bit anxious. The idea of interviewing a stream of strangers, some of whom may be perfectly suited for your coffee shop, and some who may be perfect for a job somewhere else, can be very stressful. You'll have to attract applicants, review resumes, conduct interviews, and train these individuals to run your coffee shop, and after all you've been through getting to this point, you may feel low on energy. That being said, being organized and clear about your vision and plan at this point will serve you just as well as it has in all of the previous steps.

Determine Who Does What ... and When

The absolute first step of hiring is figuring out the actual tasks that you need your employees to complete, every single day. Sit down and honestly consider who is going to be doing every single task in your coffee shop. This can include:

- Cleaning machines
- Cleaning the space, including floors, seating areas, restrooms, kitchens
- Collecting trash and taking it to the outdoor receptacle
- Collecting dishes
- Washing dishes
- Restocking supplies
- Taking orders
- Cashing out customers
- Operating age-sensitive machinery, such as slicers and ovens
- Making hot drinks

- Making cold or frozen drinks
- Serving food and beverages
- Baking any food made in-house
- Roasting coffee beans, if done in-house
- Taking inventory
- End of day accounting, including tallying receipts
- Payroll

And possibly much more, depending on the size and scope of your coffee shop. There should never be a moment in which your staff asks you "who is supposed to ____?"

As you get a feel for all of the tasks that have to be completed, both simultaneously and within the course of a business day, you may see that some tasks can be grouped together. For example, the person who is cleaning the dining area could also gather and wash the dishes. The person who is doing end-of-day accounting could also take inventory. This is the process through which you start establishing roles.

In many establishments, many of the roles are interchangeable. For example, many small restaurants and coffee shops have checklists of tasks that need to be accomplished throughout the day, which can be done by any staff member, so long as those tasks are completed in a timely manner. When it comes to emptying trash, any staff member should be able to remove the garbage bag, place it in the collection bin, and replace the trash bag. When it comes to wiping down tables or countertops, most staff members could handle that.

At the same time, there are going to be roles which require more training. The staff members who make drinks are going to need to be trained to memorize all of your various drink recipes. If you are making food from scratch, you'll need a baker who can reliably recreate recipes over and over again. The person who operates the register will have to learn the ins-and-outs of the Point of Sale system. You may wish to have only the most trustworthy employee—perhaps a manager—handle accounting and inventory.

There are, of course, distinct advantages to cross-training absolutely every employee. In smaller establishments, everyone knows how to navigate the cash register and take an order, everyone knows where all the supplies are, and everyone can at least find and follow the drink guide in order to make beverages for guests. Cross-training all of your employees is the best way to ensure you're not left in a lurch when someone is unavailable for a shift.

At the same time, it can be beneficial to create specific roles, specifically in the case of a manager role. Unless you plan to be at your coffee shop every hour of every day, you will need someone to supervise the actions at your shop. You will need a trusted resource that can answer (or find the answer to) any questions, who can confidently reduce conflict, and who can address customer concerns according to company policy on your behalf. A manager can act as your assistant in a variety of ways, which will take some of the burden of daily operations off of you so you can concentrate on keeping your business running smoothly from a budget, marketing, and product perspective.

The number of staff you hire and their roles is entirely up to you and based largely on your coffee shop and your goals, but bear in mind that budget is a part of the equation.

Hire Carefully and Confidently

Once you have established the various roles your employees will have, you'll also have an idea of how many employees you'll need on the floor at any given time. Then consider your operating hours. If your doors are open from 6 am to 9 pm, you'll have to divide up the shifts, as very few people want to work fifteen-hour days. How many shifts will you have, and how many employees per shift? It may not be the same across the board, either. This is something you might not know until you've been in operation for a while. For example, mornings might be an incredible rush, so staffing will need to be at a peak, while evenings are slower and more sedate, requiring fewer staff members. These will be things to keep in mind when planning how many staff members you'll need to hire.

In addition, you'll need to give employees a few days off per week. No one wants to work every day, and in some places, there are laws prohibiting it. So now, you'll want to calculate how many shifts you have, over how many days, and how you'll want to spread employees over those days. Again, there's no right answer, and much of this will depend on employment regulations in your area. You may be required to give employees a break after so many hours on the job, so keep things like this in mind when considering how the schedule will work.

Now you'll have an idea of how many people you need to hire to fill those shifts. One word of the wise when starting out is to hire lean, but not TOO lean. Understaffing means overworking, which leads to employees quitting out of frustration. Set the expectation early in the hiring process that you are a brand new business, and that more employees will be hired as required, but don't dangle that particular carrot in front of your staff for too long. Many people will be understanding, and as long as they are treated well and compensated for their efforts, will help put in the hard work that gets a new business up and running. At the same time, everyone has a breaking point, and "helping out" doesn't mean "running ragged."

What about salaries? Granted, this depends a great deal on the cost of living in your area. You will need to research the wage structure of nearby coffee shops in order to be competitive. You will also need to balance what you can afford to pay staff with your overall budget and monthly expenses. How about tips? Will you have a tip jar available, and if so, how will staff members split tips? You want a system that treats all workers fairly, so be careful. Lastly, what about raises and incentives? Perhaps you offer a holiday bonus for working during what are surely hectic times. You may choose to have incentives based on regular performance reviews or based on years of service.

Some new business owners have friends and family volunteer to help them out as they're getting things up and running. Depending on your friends and family, this could either be a blessing or a curse. As long as you are able to work well with the people you know, this could be a fine plan, at least for the short term. Keep roles and expectations well-defined, and make sure these volunteers are aware that you are still the boss, and things should work out at least until you've got a full staff helping you out.

Now it comes to actually finding people to apply for your staff positions! There are many ways to do this, and a lot of the process is dependent on your community. You may wish to put out ads on local Facebook groups, letting the area know you are hiring. You'll definitely want to announce job openings on your own social media and website. If you are in a larger city, you may look to post your job openings on sites like Craigslist, or even job sites like Indeed. If you're in a smaller community, you may be able to hang a few signs in strategic locations and get plenty of traffic.

When advertising your job opening, make sure you are as specific as possible about both the duties and the qualifications the ideal candidate will possess. You won't need to list absolutely every detail, for example, "daily cleaning of service area, seating area, and restrooms" should be sufficient for that particular job duty. At the same time, "making coffee" is a very vague representation of all the nuances of preparing drip coffee, pulling espresso shots, and steaming or blending. Make sure that the employees who will need to speak to customers are aware of that particular duty. It is also extremely important to note any physical qualifications at this time, such as "ability to stand for entire shift" or "ability to lift up to fifty pounds." This circles back into the ADA compliance piece as well as labor laws, so make sure prospective employees are aware before they apply if parts of their job may be physically demanding.

We recommend having every person interested in working at your coffee shop fill out an employment application. This document doesn't have to be too terribly in-depth, but will allow you to have a record of the name and general experience of every person who would like to work at your shop. This is great to have on hand any time you need to do some hiring—you can look back on these applications to start. A sample application might include:

- Full name
- Contact info (email and phone number)
- Days available
- Employment history
- References
- Related skills or experience

You may also ask for a brief cover letter or a short explanation of why they are interested in working at your coffee shop, to ensure they are actually interested in following through with the process, and not simply applying because it seemed like a good idea at the time.

You'll also need to make prospective employees aware of any pre-hire background checks, drug tests, and ServSafe certification that they'll need prior to employment. Employees must be informed of and agree to background checks if you choose to have them done. Many employers choose to make employees aware of this process before even conducting interviews. There are legal ramifications of all of these pre-employment requirements, so be sure to study up on your local requirements.

Also, bear in mind why you are doing these tests, and apply the same logic to all employees. The goal is to ensure the employees have been fully honest with you on their applications, and that you can feel at ease about having them handle your money, work face-to-face with your customers, and properly use any equipment you have that may be dangerous. This is not a witch hunt, and you may have to have a few awkward conversations with prospective employees before deciding to hire them. Above all, you want to hire good workers who will get the job done right every single day. This skill often exists beyond any past legal transgressions or a comprehensive education, so be fair and reasonable when evaluating background checks and the like.

This brings up the next thing to keep in mind: What skill set do you want your employees to have? Will you require previous coffee shop experience, or will restaurant experience suffice? If they are extremely skilled in customer service, will you take a chance in training them on how to work in a coffee shop? It's highly unlikely that you will find a full staff that knows every skill you need them to know when they walk through your doors, so decide what you are willing to train, and what skills are an absolute must-have at the offset.

Next, consider what questions you'll ask in your interviews. Remember, there are certain things you legally cannot discuss, so be careful of those topics. Your goal in an interview is to get a feel of the individual's personality, their skills, their comfort in learning new skills, and their willingness to be a team player. You might also want to test their familiarity with a few popular coffee beverages that you'll be selling. Sample questions might include:

- Why do you want to work here?
- How would you react if a customer became angry due to an incorrect order?
- What is your greatest strength? Weakness?
- What are some of the things you look forward to learning in this job?
- What experience makes you feel confident about working here?
- What is the difference between a cappuccino and a latte?

Much as you would not want to be interviewed when you are unprepared, people do not want to be interviewed by someone who is not prepared to conduct the interview. Make sure you have a clear set of questions to ask and take notes as the interview subject speaks. Again, you may not wish to hire this person now, but their information may be relevant at a later date for a future position. Schedule plenty of time in your day to conduct each interview and set aside a quiet place where you will not be interrupted during the interview. Take the time to give them a tour of the space and discuss expectations during the initial interview. While you don't have to give away the recipe to your secret mocha syrup, you will want each candidate to understand their duties and what is expected of them before they sign the employment agreement.

Do not be in such a rush to hire that you ignore red flags. This can be anything from lack of reliable transportation to work, to absolutely no coffee knowledge, to showing up to the interview in inappropriate clothing. While discrimination is strictly illegal, knowing when someone is not a good fit for your coffee shop based on their skills, capabilities, or hygiene is an important part of making good hiring decisions.

At the end of the day, only you will be able to make the call as to which candidates are best for your coffee shop, and what duties you'd like them to fulfill. As you go through the hiring process, make sure you are hiring individuals who can fit into a variety of shifts in your schedule, and who knows or can be trained on a variety of duties. This will ensure you've got enough staff and enough talent to lift your coffee shop into success!

Learning All There is to Know

Eventually, if all goes well and your staff expands according to your vision and plan, someone else will be doing the training. But before your coffee shop opens for its very first day of business, only one person knows how you want things done: YOU!

All businesses should have an Employee Handbook, no matter how basic. This will include things like policies and procedures which will answer all questions, from "what if I can't make my shift" to "how do I request a day off?" You'll want to address sexual harassment, on-the-job injuries, opening procedures, closing procedures, what to do in an emergency, in the event of a fire, in the event of extreme weather, and more. Establishing expectations is the basis of training.

You'll also want a Training Handbook. This will include things like instructions for using all of the equipment, recipes for drinks, instructions for assembling and plating food, as well as the frequency and procedure for cleaning, and more.

The idea of having both the Employee Handbook and the Training Handbook is that you are establishing without a doubt what expectations, duties, roles, and responsibilities belong to whom. In the event of an accident, injury, or incident, you do not want to be caught with any ambiguity or loose ends that could result in a lawsuit or other legal action. Again, this is an area where you may wish to consult with a Human Resources expert or lawyer to make sure you haven't left anything to chance.

You may prefer to schedule one-on-one training with your new staff members, or you may wish to get them together as a group. There are advantages to each, of course, and since you may conduct more than one training session, you might choose to have both types of training sessions. Walk employees through the process of making a drink to your specifications. Let them enter orders on the new Point Of Sale system, or POS. Make up mock orders so they can test each other on their knowledge and the process. Make sure they have a firm grasp of their duties and are confident that they know where they can find information and answers. You may wish to have copies of the handbooks available in the service areas, especially just after you've opened. After all, this is new to everyone. Make it as easy as possible for employees to find the answers and arm them with the information they need to be competent and confident in their jobs.

Walk through the menu. Make sure ingredient lists and recipes are posted where your staff members can easily access them. Make sure these notes are laminated and well bound so they don't wander off or get stained beyond recognition. While it may take a few days for your staff to know the menu by heart, they should be able to guide customers through understanding the difference between item X and item Y on the very first day, even if they have to look it up.

Lastly, consider your employment terms. Most businesses have a training period or probation period, during which time a new staff member is expected to learn everything they need to know—or how and where to find the answer to an obscure question. How long will your probation period be? What is the incentive to completing the probationary period? Will the employees get a boost in salary? An employee discount? Small incentives are helpful in giving employees a clear goal for performing well during the probationary period and beyond.

Be Demanding

You are also in charge of determining what kind of boss you're going to be. Are you going to be hands-on, pitching in when your staff gets overwhelmed? Are you going to be strictly a long-distance boss, in your off-site office until someone calls? Are you going to be intensely "in the trenches" with your employees at first, until everyone has a feel for how the shop is going to run? While everyone has a different management style, as the owner of a business you'll need to set roles, responsibilities, and limitations for yourself, as well.

What will be your discipline style? Many businesses use a "verbal warning, written warning, probation, termination" progression, in which each transgression is addressed with increasingly serious consequences. Then again, what if the error was completely unintentional? How will you mediate disagreements between employees? What sort of actions will lead to disciplinary action, versus a basic re-training conversation? All of this information will need to be in the Employee Handbook, but as the owner of the establishment, it is up to you to enforce all of these policies equally and fairly.

What day-to-day expectations do you have for your staff? Perhaps you expect them to show up ten minutes before their shift, dressed in uniform, and ready to clock in for the day. Who pays for the uniform? Who cleans the uniform? Do they wear name tags? What happens if they lose their name tags? Depending on the materials involved, it might be costly to replace a name tag.

Performance reviews are another place where you will need to practice being demanding. Coaching and feedback should not demean a worker or make them feel like they are incompetent; rather, they should feel like they are being empowered with the information that will take them to the next level in their personal success. Decide when you are going to have performance reviews and stick to that schedule. You may wish to start at the conclusion of the probationary period, each quarter, or annually. Make sure you hold all employees to the same regularity of reviews and hold each employee equally accountable for both their own and the overall business's success.

Furthermore, do not wait for a performance review to discuss concerns or give praise you may have for your staff. Especially in the case of concerns, the actions of your staff may have a negative impact on the overall success of your coffee shop. If another staff member reports questionable actions, or you observe it yourself, investigate and discuss it with that employee in a neutral manner. Remember: miscommunication and misunderstandings are very real things. The only way to resolve these errors is to discuss them calmly in an environment of education, not accusation.

These may seem like micromanaging-level details, but they are truly required considerations when managing staff. There are many, many things to keep in mind as an employer. Many of your actions can and will have legal ramifications. They'll also have personal repercussions. The first time you have to terminate an employee, it will feel awful for everyone involved. Make sure that you are armed with a plan that meets all of the state and federal legal regulations, and be prepared for every eventuality. You might feel oddly paranoid and out of your element, so feel free to seek professional employment guidance, but rest assured that knowing how to handle a situation will make it easier to follow through in the event that you really need to do so.

Of course, you want to be kind and fair, but just like any setting, there will be rules that must be followed, or consequences will ensue. You will best serve the success of your company if you are fair, yet demanding. Respectful, yet unwavering. Empathetic, but not pathetic. As the owner of this coffee shop, you are the leader. You should both command and deserve respect.

Step 8: Planning for the Big Day

At this point, your vision has become a reality. You've enacted a plan from square one. You've got a perfect, well-groomed space, from which you're going to sell your carefully curated collection of coffee and more. The scene is set, the beans are ground, and the staff is eager to serve their first customer. This is the moment you've been waiting for!

Setting the Stage

There's one last thing you need to do before you let customers in: set the menu and the prices. You'll want to make sure the menu is prominently displayed—no one likes to guess at what you serve and how much it costs.

When it comes to creating a menu, make sure it is legible in every way. Make sure the spelling and punctuation are correct. Make sure the wording is large and clear. Make sure any interesting ingredients or notes are available for customers to consider. Some cafes have large menus posted overhead for customers to read, and small handheld or paper menus where they can read more about flavors and aroma notes. Customers will need to be aware of what they should expect when they take that first sip, so these notes will help set those expectations.

Depending on your anticipated clientele, you may want to avoid being too creative with the naming of your beverages as well. Using the banana-and-chocolate example from earlier, consider whether your customers will be comfortable ordering a "Bananafanana-fo-foffee," or if something like "Mocha Banana Royale" both accurately describes the drink while being accessible to your audience. Make sure drink names actually relate to the drink, as well. Being too creative can lead to more questions, and if you're looking to have a rush of customers seeking that morning hit of caffeine, they'll be less likely to want to ask questions and do research. They just want a delicious drink in their hands before they face another busy day.

Pricing... is a delicate matter, to say the least. The price of coffee varies so widely that the coffee shop model is often used in business classes. A lot of factors will dictate your pricing, especially the going rate of coffee in your area. Try to stay in the same range as your direct competitors, as this will encourage people that your product is just as much of a value as other cafes in the area. All that said, though, your pricing should include:

- Cost of coffee
- Cost of labor
- Cost of takeaway cup and lid
- Cost of any additional ingredients
- Cost of any cream/sugar/etc

All of these costs can be calculated from the business accounts you've been tracking diligently through this entire process. Calculating the cost of supplies will be the easiest part since this likely does not waiver. A cup of house blend will require a certain portion of a bag of beans. If you pay $10 for a bag of beans, and a cup of house blend requires 1/100th of a bag of beans, then your cost for that cup of coffee is 10 cents. To determine labor, consider how long it takes to actually prepare and serve that drink, compared to the worker's hourly salary.

Then, on top of this, determine what you want your profit margin to be. You can certainly visit the accountant again if this part is confusing. Altogether, the profit margin should be enough to pay for all of your supplies, ingredients, staff, rent/mortgage, loan, and a bit for yourself. The profit margin may not be the same for every customer and every drink. For example, a customer who has a drink "for here," will not need the takeaway cup and lid. A customer who drinks their coffee plain will not incur the costs for cream and sugar. You won't charge them differently, however. That would be far too complicated at the outset. Instead, when you're calculating profit margin, you'll expect that a portion of customers will make you a little less profit than others.

At this point, you may feel completely confused by the entire game and wish to rush through this process. Do not give in to this temptation. Simply stay calm and do the math ... or pay your accountant to do so.

The Final Walkthrough

Before you even consider opening, make sure you have scheduled all of your final requirements. Make sure all of your deliveries have been scheduled appropriately so that they don't overlap, but that all of your supplies and products arrive on time. You'll need time to get all of the storage containers sanitized and ready to use. You'll need to make sure any refrigeration has been inspected and cleared for use. Your local ordinances may require a final walkthrough of the building before issuing your building and business permits. You'll need time to make sure uniforms are cleaned and pressed, furniture assembled and cleaned, artwork hung, and music playlists sorted.

There should be one final, peaceful moment in between all the last-minute melee where you have the ability to walk through one final time before opening. Take full advantage of this moment. For the past several months, you have been engulfed in your coffee shop from the standpoint of an owner. Any time you've looked at the setting, you've looked at it with the careful gaze of someone who needs to make sure everything is perfect and in the most correct spot.

Now, take the time to look at it as a connoisseur. Sit in a chair and think of how a customer will feel at your cafe. This is the final moment for last-minute adjustments, so let everything soak in. Is the lighting at the right level of brightness? Is the music too loud or too soft? When the machinery is working, is it obnoxiously loud? Is the smell of coffee too strong, or just right? This is your last chance to make modifications to anything, from acoustics to the seating layout. Use this time wisely to ensure everything meets that original vision and plan.

The next few sections will include some tips for both a soft opening and a Grand Opening. These are included to help guide you through the process. You may choose to go a completely different direction for your coffee shop, based on your experience, comfort, community, and more. That is absolutely fine. If you are looking to celebrate the opening of your new cafe in a big way, or just need some tips for drawing a crowd right off the bat, read on!

Planning Your Grand Opening

Many cafes and restaurant owners like to do a quiet, "soft" opening before their official, public Grand Opening. Having some form of a soft opening allows you to shake out any last-minute wrinkles before the general public is allowed to stop by, so if there's a drink recipe that needs tweaking or any gaps in the service flow amongst staff members, this is a great time to address them.

Sometimes this takes the form of an invite-only event, in which your team is cordially invited to visit your coffee shop for a grand reveal. This could include anyone who has made this dream a reality, including your friends, family, accountant, contractors, designers, landlord or realty agent, lawyer, marketing assistants, your staff's friends and family, investors… the list can go on and on. Having a quiet reveal party like this will be a warm "thank you" for all of the help these folks have provided to you.

You may also wish to casually open the doors before the grand opening and see who wanders in. This form of a soft opening allows you additional training opportunities for staff—they get to actually serve real guests, but everyone understands this is not the full out and formal experience.

Once you choose the date for your Grand Opening, it is set in stone in the eyes of the community, so be absolutely sure you're ready to go. If you're going to put it on your menu, it should be available. The staff should be in uniform, trained, and prepared. The dishes should be spotless and neatly stacked, and that shiny gleam of newness should greet each brand new patron.

If you are anything less than completely ready, do not proceed. Here are some things to check off before you unlock that door to the public:

1. Do you have all the ingredients for all of your drinks and snacks?
2. Do you have a tidy, attractive way to serve them all?
3. Is the POS system working correctly?
4. Do you have change to give guests who pay in cash?
5. Is the staff fully trained on when to serve, clean, assemble, etc?
6. Is everyone in uniform, ready to greet customers warmly?
7. Are all of the fixtures and furnishings installed and ready to be used?
8. Are there any signs of construction (wires, pipes, drywall, sheeting, etc)?
9. Are the restrooms fully stocked and functional?
10. Does the parking lot look attractive and safe?

If you can answer YES to all of these questions, you are ready for your Grand Opening!

What Will Make Your Day Special?

Your first day of business will undoubtedly be very special for you and your staff. After all, you've been working toward this magical moment for as long as you can remember! In order to encourage more people to come out to your Grand Opening, it's a good idea to do something special to celebrate the day.

This, of course, can take many shapes, depending on the focus of your coffee shop and your community. If your vision was around a meeting place for artistic and creative types, maybe you have an exhibition of local artists to coincide with your first official day of business. If you're going with the "gourmet experience" type of coffee shop, perhaps you pull out a very rare and special bean for the big day. You can invite local celebrities, have the local radio station attend … whatever will get the word out in your specific area and draw attention to your fabulous new business in a positive way can be a great way to start off your new venture.

Remember, of course, that there will be hiccups along the way—things likely won't always go as planned. Just like any big event, the weather may not cooperate, something technical will fail, and you'll have to come up with a workaround. Breathe deeply and go with the flow. Short of having to cancel the entire thing, a well-entertained and pleased crowd will also go with the flow and appreciate that you don't have control over everything.

If you are going to plan things like celebrities, musical performances, a ceremony with the mayor, and the like, make sure you plan out the day's schedule well beforehand, with a significant amount of padding in between events. You will not want to be rushed, as you may have minor catastrophes to attend to throughout the course of the day. Have plenty of time for things to flow out, with your new beverages and snacks taking center stage any time there's a break in the action.

It's also a great idea to announce your Grand Opening anywhere possible. Going back to the marketing plans, make sure your Grand Opening celebration is posted on your website. Include a count-down clock, if you wish. People get excited when they're given a specific time frame for an event, so encourage it! Get people hyped on your social media accounts and add your event information to any local event page that will have it. You may have to pay a small fee to have it added to local news event calendars, but a small fee could be recouped in just a few sales, so it will likely be worth it.

Put up signs as you're permitted—at places where the public congregates, along the road, in front of your door. Scream from the mountaintops if you wish—just make sure you do everything to make sure as many people as possible know about your event!

Special Deals for a Special Day

You might have seen businesses that offer a special coupon that's good for Opening Day only. These are the types of flyers you might see on your car windshield or stuffed in a mailbox. There are both good and not-so-good things about special offers on a Grand Opening day. While you are definitely likely to entice customers to come in and use that coupon, you will be selling product at a reduced rate, and you will have to pay for the flyers to be printed. Plus, there's the matter of distributing them in the first place.

Instead, you may wish to offer a very special drink that's ONLY available on Opening Day. Many people find it very hard to resist a limited time offer. You can also serve something special, such as a free piece of "birthday" cake while supplies last. You want to encourage people to fall in love with your product, but you don't want your Grand Opening to drive you further into debt. Free small samples are a good option, as they are often low-cost and low-waste, while demonstrating your amazing product. Also, as the business owner, remember not to get caught up in the excitement and give away the proverbial farm.

Consider, however, having coupons at your register, or handing them out to people in person at your Grand Opening event. This will encourage them to come back a second time, to spend even more money, and become impressed with you all over again. Make sure your social media and web address are prominently displayed, and hint that you'll be making future special offers there. That will encourage people to follow you on social media, which will keep your business name fresh in their minds every time they check their feed.

What Do You Need When You Need a Helper?

This may come as a shock, but you will not be able to run your Grand Opening alone. The coffee grinder will choose this moment to become stuck. The phone will ring off the hook. Someone will need to take care of traffic in the parking lot. Your star barista will suddenly blank on what goes into your signature drink. Something will drop and spill and require immediate cleanup.

You would do well to have your entire staff on hand during the Grand Opening. It will be an incredible learning experience that they can all reference, going forward. They'll be able to help each other out with the learning curve. Just make sure they don't all get in each other's way, so shift out and rotate as necessary.

You may also wish to have a few volunteers for this event. These can be team members, friends and family, or local volunteers who are willing to come out for the day to make sure no one double-parks. Whatever you choose, make sure these individuals are well-informed in their duties, and where to find you in case things get out of hand.

Due to high-traffic concerns, you may also need to alert the local emergency services of your Grand Opening, especially if you're expecting a big crowd. Check your local ordinances, because it would be the ultimate bummer to have your party shut down due to an avoidable violation.

Once your team is assembled, make sure you have time to rehearse everything. Make sure everyone knows where everything is located, and that roles and duties for this special day are carefully defined. The last thing you need is drama between two parties of overzealous volunteers! Doing anything last minute is unavoidable, but make sure the largest moving pieces of the grand opening are addressed long before the first customer pulls into the parking lot.

Be Prepared

Lastly, remember that this is the first day of the rest of your life. Maybe it won't be the raging bash you thought it was going to be. Maybe it snows. Maybe someone trips in the parking lot and injures themselves. Do not go into panic mode.

Have everything rehearsed and ready to go. Extra electrical extension cords. Duct tape for miles. Beans at the ready, and towers of to-go cups. It may feel a bit like you're going into battle, and in a sense, you are. You are conquering this community on behalf of your coffee shop.

Furthermore, be prepared for things to go wrong, as mentioned earlier. Having things like walkie-talkies, or cell phones within reach, will help you and everyone helping you run the event communicate, especially if the setting is noisy or the locations too far apart to shout. Walk through and rehearse how things should go, and make sure everyone is aware of where the phones, extra supplies, first aid kit, and additional stock will be located. Stage everything for success, too. For example, if trash bags are normally kept under the counter in a cabinet, perhaps they can be placed in a cabinet closer to the trash cans for today. Maybe instead of happily being locked away in the office, register tape sits next to the register today, so it can easily be changed in between customers. Plan for super-hyper-efficiency. You only get one chance to make a first impression!

No matter what happens the first day, learn and move on. Any mistakes are hereby considered "learning experiences." Anything that doesn't work out quite right will be assessed and reviewed. Whatever the weak link is, become bolder and better. As we've mentioned several times, building a business starts with a vision and a plan, but it is a continual process to keep that vision and plan fresh and viable and running smoothly.

Business as Usual

And just like that, it has finally happened. What started many long months or years ago as a vision and a plan has become a full-fledged coffee shop. Your hard work has paid off. All of those moments of anger, frustration, and sadness, of feeling overwhelmed and under-prepared ... all of them have led to the moment when you can reach over your counter, hand a customer their order, and say, "Thank you for stopping at my coffee shop today."

Every day will be a different day. Some days you will panic about customers and money. Some days you will be fully in the weeds, wondering when you'll have time to restock the coffee bar or take out the trash. After a brilliant opening period, you'll start to learn what "normal" business looks like for your cafe. You'll learn the names of the regulars. You know when the rushes come. You'll understand which drinks sell like crazy, and which are terrific flops.

As time goes by, you'll learn more about your business, and become more and more comfortable with the ins and outs of the business decisions. You'll get inventory needs down to a science and the menu down to an art. Don't ever be afraid to make adjustments, but as any keen person in sales and marketing will tell you, don't get rid of your biggest hits.

Perhaps, as the years go by, you'll be interested in expanding your wildly popular brand. Perhaps you'll play it safe and stay with the tried-and-true method that is serving you well today. You may wish to try out new ideas, new recipes, new events, but remember, the success you are experiencing now is based on what you are doing now. Anything that doesn't work now will continue to not work well unless it is adjusted.

Coaching and feedback are not only useful for your staff, but for you, as well. Stay connected to your customers. Learn what they love and don't love about your shop. Respond to their needs—don't ignore complaints and concerns. Encourage communication from your customers, because that will help you know what they enjoy about your shop. Remember, you are essentially running this business for them. Without customers, there are no sales, and with no sales, there's no cafe!

Every day that you open the doors for business, let yourself feel fulfilled by the vision and plan that started this whole thing. Let yourself feel pride for a job well done, and for making it through one of the most intense processes of your life. Think back on how you navigated the budget. What issues you encountered when finding the location and preparing it. The trials and tribulations that went into choosing your menu. We encourage you to keep all of your notes from the process. Those rejected recipes might come through as a new favorite someday! Furthermore, those small pieces of the dream that didn't make it into your coffee shop's first iteration may someday be incorporated into a remodel or refresh. Don't put everything to bed—instead, collect and relish your memories. These are the daydreams that came true.

Conclusion

We hope you have enjoyed this journey through the basic process of opening your own coffee shop. Whether you're staring at a cup of hot joe right now, thinking how ready you are to start the process, or if you're trying to decide if that's the caffeine jitters or a serious case of nerves, we hope that the information presented here gives you a sense of what you'll need to keep in mind when opening your flagship cafe.

Please bear in mind that this is to be considered as a general guide for opening your own coffee shop. As we stated in the beginning, it was written with the standards of practice for the United States in mind. Each state has tons of different requirements and regulations on all of the aspects of running a business; in fact, there are so many, we could write a book for each state. Therefore, we tried to keep things simple and streamlined, but you will absolutely need to check with the state regulations before setting up your own business. We have included some helpful links in the index to get you started on the research path, but remember, regulations change quickly, so you may wish to consult with a professional to ensure everything you're doing and all of your practices are legal, correct, and accurate.

As we've stated several times in this book, there are times in which it is best to get a professional's advice. Leaving things to chance is never recommended. Asking for help is never a bad thing. While this book is intended to set you on a solid path of considerations and options when opening your own coffee shop, there's no way we can anticipate every situation you may encounter on your own path. In fact, there may be times the professionals on your team even say, "Wow, we did not see that coming!"

We encourage you to take a look at some of the links in the index for further guidance. We hope that you'll be filled with inspiration and motivation to consider research that is more personalized to your very own coffee shop. None of the links we have included are intended to be endorsements, but rather examples of some of the resources that are out there.

This book required significant research, and the words of wisdom of many experts in many different fields have been incorporated into each chapter. As you proceed down the path of opening your own cafe, consider building your own team of mentors. Interview people in the local food scene. Get a feel for what works for them and what doesn't. Join professional groups—both in person and on social media—now. Start obsessively visiting coffee shops everywhere you go. Make notes about how things vary in your neighborhood from spots in other towns, cities, states, and so on. This is going to be your hard-earned dream come true, so gather your allies and keep yourself informed!

Congratulations on your choice to pursue your own business. You deserve plenty of praise for your dedication to your vision and your plan. We hope your business thrives and flourishes, and that you someday are able to pass your own words of wisdom down to the next generation of local entrepreneurs!

HOW TO MAKE COFFEE YOUR BUSINESS.

Index

As noted throughout the text, here are a few helpful links we've collected to inspire you. These are grouped by topic, so you can choose the sections and areas that might best help you at each stage in the process.

Legal Considerations

The following links will guide you to Federal and State websites that outline a variety of health, safety, employment, and discrimination requirements. It is highly recommended that you give each of these a thorough read before even starting the process of creating a business plan. This list is not all-inclusive; however, you will be led through a variety of points and considerations when gauging all of the legal requirements that govern your location.

OSHA: Occupational Health and Safety Administration. This agency exists within the United States Department of Labor and works to ensure proper and safe working conditions for all.
https://www.osha.gov/SLTC/restaurant/standards.html
https://www.osha.gov/SLTC/foodbornedisease/standards.html)

FDA: The Food and Drug Administration is a federal agency within the United States Department of Health and Human Services, protecting the health of the public with regulations that ensure the safety of food and food supplies.
https://www.fda.gov/food/fda-food-code/state-retail-and-food-service-codes-and-regulations-state

ADA: The Americans With Disabilities Act is a civil rights law that prohibits any kind of discrimination based on disability. ADA Compliance is granted by adhering to a number of regulations that cover everything from public accommodations to employment.
https://www.ada.gov/smbustxt.htm

ServSafe: a program administered by the National Restaurant Association that provides sanitation certification that is required for many in the food industry.
https://www.servsafe.com/ServSafe-Food-Handler/Buy-Handler-Products?gclid=CjoKC-Qjw6eTtBRDdARIsANZWjYa1BP3ynkJLinuDteqwvhTw6t4cv-0giwD_nCjAZQGhgKpBZRQ-6J2kaAhDeEALw_wcB

State Health Departments: This list helps you locate your state health department for information about requirements that are specific to your state.
https://healthfinder.gov/FindServices/SearchContext.aspx?topic=820&show=1

US Department of Labor: These links will help you discover the Federal laws and regulations surrounding safely and legally hiring and maintaining employment for your new staff.
https://www.dol.gov/general/aboutdol/majorlaws,   https://www.usa.gov/labor-laws,
https://www.dol.gov/general/location

EEOC: The United States Equal Employment Opportunity Commission has also issued a series of laws and regulations, which can help you avoid unintentional discrimination.
https://www.eeoc.gov/laws/practices/

IRS: Internal Revenue Service, which handles employment taxes and all of the forms required when hiring a new employee.
https://www.irs.gov/businesses/small-businesses-self-employed/hiring-employees

Employment Lawyer: This resource can help you avoid and remove yourself legally from possible predicaments you may encounter when setting up your employees and practices.
http://www.myemploymentlawyer.com/

Financial Links

In Step 2, we mention a few sources for funding and gathering investors. The following sites were mentioned in that chapter, so we have linked them here. You may also wish to talk to agents and specialists at local banks, credit unions, and other financial institutions. Interest rates and loan requirements will vary from location to location, so shopping around will help you gauge the best option for you and your budget.

Small Business Association: Support and connections for entrepreneurs wading into the waters of starting a small business.
https://www.sba.gov/

Swift Capital: Another resource specializing in connecting small business owners with funding.
https://www.swiftcapital.com/

Prosper, TrustLeaf, OnDeck, and Lending Club: Connections to investors and lenders for your area, your business, and your ideas.

www.prosper.com

https://www.facebook.com/trustleaf/

www.ondeck.com

www.lendingclub.com

National Business Incubation Association: A global network of incubators, entrepreneurs, accelerators, and mentors for new business owners.

https://inbia.org/

Angel Networks: Groups of investors and entrepreneurs established with the sole goal of helping up-and-coming business owners with financial and practical support.

https://www.angelcapitalassociation.org/

https://www.angelinvestmentnetwork.us/

Crowdfunding: Websites that allow interested, independent parties to make donations to your cause. Be sure to read their rules and requirements before setting up your account!

www.kickstarter.com

www.ourcrowd.com

www.indiegogo.com

Technology

We mentioned a few ways in which technology can aid you in staying organized. We also mentioned sites that can help you with marketing, such as creating a logo and a webpage.

Floor plan creation and simulation: These programs can help you enter measurements to create your perfect floor plan, allowing you to accurately fit all of the furnishings and fixtures in all the right spots.

https://floorplancreator.net/

https://www.smartdraw.com/floor-plan/floor-plan-designer.htm

https://floorplanner.com/

Logo Creation: These sites can help you dream up your idea logo, either for a small fee, or completely free!

https://www.wix.com/logo/maker

https://placeit.net/logo-maker
https://www.freelogodesign.org/

Website: We mentioned WordPress as a possible website tool. Here's a link to learn more about their services.
https://wordpress.com/

Supply Chain

Please note that not all of these suppliers will contract with every location or every type of business. These links are intended as a launchpad for reviewing possibilities in your area and for your specific cafe. Additionally, many of these suppliers offer a variety of services that go beyond their listing in the directory below.

Uniforms, Linens, Sanitation: These vendors offer a variety of services that help keep your cafe clean and up to code. Some offer a very wide variety of services, including inventory and more, so take a look at all each one has to offer.
https://www.cintas.com/facilityservices/
https://www.sysco.com/
https://www.therdstore.com/

Equipment Specific to Coffee Shops and Cafes: For your espresso machines, grinders, drip brew, and more, it's best to start with experts. These companies market specifically to coffee shop owners and those who sell large quantities of professional-grade coffee.
https://www.webstaurantstore.com/restaurant-equipment.html   https://www.coffeeam.com/wholesale-1/cafe-equipment-packages.html   https://www.voltagerestaurantsupply.com/

Coffee Beans and Supplies: Exotic, gourmet, delicious, and more. These vendors specialize in coffee beans for coffee shops. When purchasing your beans, make sure you're not settling for anything you wouldn't like to be sold yourself!
https://www.kaldi.com/wholesale-coffee   https://www.coffeeam.com/wholesale-1/wholesale-coffee.html
https://www.specialtyjava.com/wholesale.htm

Food, Food Supplies, Ingredients: These vendors can set you up with regular deliveries of the food, food supplies, and ingredients that will keep you in business. Many of these suppliers also have physical storefronts you can visit, to get a feel for their product and quality. Check out their websites for more information.

https://www.sysco.com/

https://www.foodservicedirect.com/

https://www.foodsupply.com/

https://www.gfs.com/en-us

www.usfoods.com

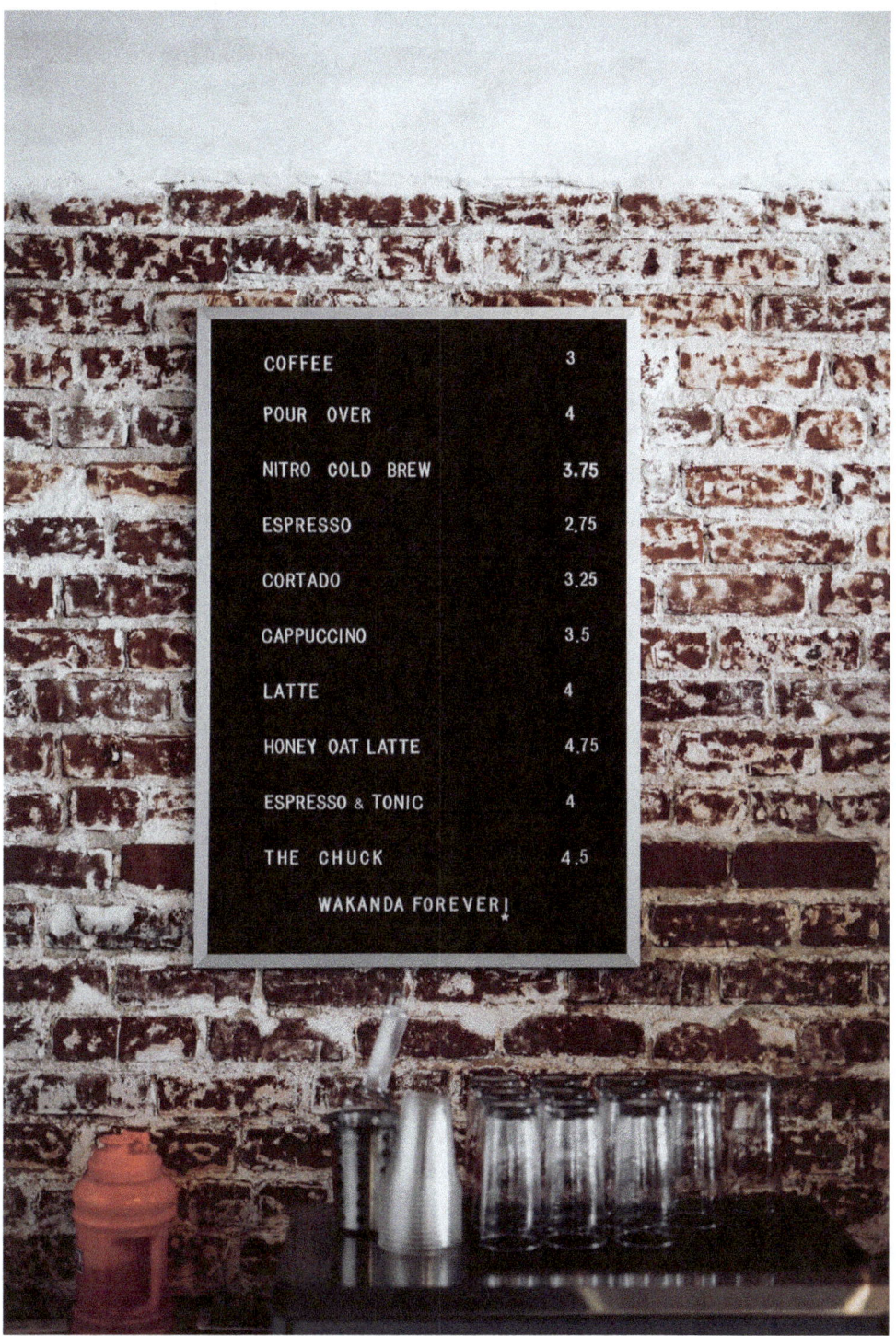

Reviews

Reviews and feedback help improve this book and the author. If you enjoy this book, we would greatly appreciate it if you could take a few moments to share your opinion and post a review on Amazon.

© 2019

www.ingramcontent.com/pod-product-compliance
Lightning Source LLC
Chambersburg PA
CBHW071236070526
44583CB00017B/2200